HOPE FOR WILDLIFE

True Stories of Animal Rescue

Ray MacLeod

NIMBUS
PUBLISHING LTD

Nimbus Publishing Limited
3731 Mackintosh St, Halifax, NS, B3K 5A5
(902) 455-4286 nimbus.ca

Printed and bound in China

Design: Jenn Embree
Author photo: Eva Mari S. Gundersen

Library and Archives Canada Cataloguing in Publication

MacLeod, Ray
Hope for Wildlife : true stories of animal rescue / Ray MacLeod.
ISBN 978-1-55109-817-3

1. Hope for Wildlife Society. 2. Wildlife rescue—Nova Scotia. 3. Animal rescue—Nova Scotia. I. Title.

QL83.2.M33 2011   639.9'609716   C2010-908129-3

We acknowledge the financial support of the Government of Canada through the Book Publishing Industry Development Program (BPIDP) and the Canada Council, and of the Province of Nova Scotia through the Department of Tourism, Culture and Heritage for our publishing activities.

To Joanne, because she believed

TABLE OF CONTENTS

FOREWORD

When I first contemplated a book being written about Hope for Wildlife, I was both excited and anxious. It's not that I didn't want the stories shared—part of Hope for Wildlife's mission is to connect people to wildlife in a positive way through knowledge and understanding. The stories in this book give people the chance to bond to each of these animals: to see their beauty, their intelligence, and their triumphs. But the stories also reveal the realities of working with wildlife: the tragedies, the mistakes, and the heartaches.

Fortunately, despite the sad stories, there are many happy endings as well. Every day we are inspired by the animals we care for, amazed by their intelligence, and astounded by their resiliency. Every case is a new challenge, an opportunity to learn, and a chance to make a difference, one animal at a time.

My wish is that you read this book with an open mind and heart; that you step inside the animals' world and discover the influence and power we as people have on them. I hope that these stories can help you take a small step in the right direction. As much as our work is about healing wildlife, it's also about healing the human spirit.

Hope for Wildlife is happy to be given the opportunity to share these stories. I hope they inspire you as much as the animals have inspired us.

Hope Swinimer
Director, Hope for Wildlife

INTRODUCTION

This is a book about wild things in peril and what people have done to help them. It is also the story of a remarkable woman and the organization she founded to provide that help. In it are many successes, a few tragic failures, and chapters that finish somewhere in between or have no end at all. Whatever the outcome, there is always hope. It is the one force that runs through every page, the talisman that gives magic to each tale.

It all began in 1997 when Hope Swinimer founded The Eastern Shore Wildlife Rehabilitation and Rescue Centre. In 2005, the name was changed to Hope for Wildlife Society, and to avoid confusion, that is what it is called in this book. Work done out of the organization's Seaforth base has helped birds, animals, and other wild creatures from every part of Nova Scotia and earned Swinimer the Canadian Wildlife Federation's 2008 Roland Michener Award for outstanding achievement in Canadian conservation.

The society is both a group of volunteers and a charity built around those volunteers to help finance their cause. This book takes you inside work with orphaned foxes and injured eagles. It introduces a blind raccoon and a doomed moose. There are stories of a car-crushed turtle that lived, but a spoiled deer that did not. Hope comes to a young bobcat someone mistook for a domestic kitten. An owl that collided with a salt truck gets a new face and another chance at life.

Through everything at Hope for Wildlife run the beliefs of its founder. Hope Swinimer is passionate in all she does, and has given herself a lot to do. Swinimer is a certified veterinary practice manager and holds a full-time job as administrator of the Dartmouth Veterinary Hospital. She recently took over the Halifax city animal pound service, founding Homeward Bound City Pound to run it. Groups all over the province constantly ask her to speak or to lead tours of her Seaforth facility. Universities have sent students, sometimes entire classes, to see how wildlife rehabilitation should be done.

Swinimer's work has made her a larger-than-life figure in Nova Scotia, a person whose name and organization are touchstones for care of the province's wild creatures. Hope for Wildlife is a continuing story with many chapters, including tales that were told, and retold, long before they were discovered by the media or printed here.

One of the reasons Hope Swinimer and her followers attract so much interest is that their adventures tend to start off in one direction, then go in another. For example, when she took the job as administrator for the Dartmouth Veterinary Hospital, Swinimer had no intention of getting involved with wildlife. Hers was to be a life of cats, dogs, and other domestic animals that people keep as pets and companions. These were the ones her doctors worked with. These were also the ones whose owners paid the bills. However, she found herself more and more drawn to injuries veterinarians did not deal with, such as the backyard blue jay that collided with a window or the porcupine with legs broken by a pickup truck.

One day in 1993, a couple who had run over a skunk brought it to Swinimer's workplace. The veterinarians could not look after the animal so she decided to take it home and do it herself, and that was how her wildlife rehabilitation started. Under her care, the skunk recovered, but was blind in one eye and could not be released. Instead, Swinimer decided to use the animal she called Zorro to teach Nova Scotians about their native wildlife. Of course, to prepare a skunk to meet the public, it had to be de-scented, which segued into the unexpected element of this tale, the part people still talk about in veterinary circles when the topic of skunk surgery is evoked.

Swinimer decided Zorro's anal musk glands had to be removed, and found no veterinarian willing to help. Finally, she badgered Dr. Ian McKay at her hospital to try. People would learn in time

Zorro, Hope Swinimer's first rehabilitated animal, is a legend at the Dartmouth Veterinary Hospital and in a certain veterinarian's household. Who knew musk glands were worse out than in?

that letting Hope Swinimer talk them into things could have unforeseen results. McKay agreed to do the de-scenting despite warnings from his colleagues.

A skunk's scent glands may be situated similar to a dog's, but they are much larger, about the size of two very large grapes, compared to the pea-sized canine ones, and much more potent. McKay worked carefully. He got the glands out without nicking them, which was his biggest fear and the subject of endless warnings, then secured the ducts to prevent any leakage. There was a slight aroma in the operating room, but no one out in the waiting area of the hospital was complaining. Swinimer and McKay declared it a success.

"I got them both out, intact, and they were sitting on a tray while I finished sewing Zorro and let him wake up. I was quite pleased, very proud of myself. I'd done it, we'd got along fine, and Zorro had lived through the surgery. We hadn't contaminated the hospital, and things were looking pretty good," said McKay.

The chickens should not yet have been counted. Another staff veterinarian entered and asked how large a skunk's musk glands were, and McKay proudly extended the tray to show him. Both

Meet Hope Swinimer and the pine marten Gretel. In 2002, Swinimer faced arrest over her little friend. For details, see chapter 4.

glands rolled off. McKay said it was like a car accident, when everything goes into slow motion and eternity passes as your vehicle swerves across the road and hits another. It seemed to take at least five minutes for the glands to roll off the tray and hit the floor.

"Then it was kind of like an atomic bomb blast," he said. "I can still see those things hitting and exploding into a mushroom arc. The odour was just incredible. It was so strong, not at all like driving by a dead skunk on the road. That would be mild by comparison. They exploded like balloons full of water, and the smell filled the hospital almost instantly. People weren't happy with me. They weren't happy with Hope. It was bad."

The entire Dartmouth Veterinary Hospital had to be evacuated and scrubbed out, inch by inch. McKay was strongly advised to shed his clothes and either bury or burn the lot, but he insisted on taking them home and trying to wash out the scent in the family laundry. Nothing good came of that. The clothing still reeked and the aroma had happily invaded his entire house. His wife arrived home from a trip a few days later and, despite an entire weekend of his frantic deodourizing, immediately asked her sheepish husband how the skunk had got in.

So there it was, the first story of many. The legend of Hope Swinimer and the strange things that happened to her and her band

Sarah Snow and Laura MacDougall look after an orphaned raccoon. Volunteers are the backbone of Hope for Wildlife.

of wildlife workers was underway, and would keep growing. Tales of glorious success and heart-wrenching failure, often couched in irony, spread year by year from there. Before long, Hope for Wildlife was rehabilitating and releasing more than 1,500 animals each year. In doing so, word of its work spread, and young people in particular found enchantment in it. For many, contact with Hope and her animals helped form their futures.

Lower Sackville's Tiffany Sullivan was one of these. In 1995, when she was twelve, a friend invited her to supper in Eastern Passage, where she could meet her friend's father's unusual girlfriend. They were eating pizza at Swinimer's kitchen table when it happened.

"I felt something on my foot and looked down. I'm pretty sure I screamed and jumped up on a chair because I'd never seen a skunk in someone's house before," Sullivan said. "It was the first wildlife I'd ever been close to. It kind of scared me a little bit."

Swinimer quickly intervened and went into education mode.

"First she said he just wanted the onions off my pizza, so I gave him those. Then she started to tell me all about wildlife, that Zorro was injured and couldn't go back."

It was Swinimer's first year, even before she'd moved to Seaforth, but her Eastern Passage home cradled the idea that would grow into Hope for Wildlife. Sullivan remembers Swinimer's backyard and just how small things were in the beginning.

"Hope had just started rehabilitation, and she had four of those chain-link dog pens. There were a fox, a raccoon, and some other little stuff," she said.

Swinimer explained how wild creatures sometimes got injured and needed human help, but the concept was entirely new to a suburban twelve year old whose closest prior contact with wildlife was watching roadkill flash by her car window.

"Before that, I never really thought about it. You'd see dead animals on the side of the road, and I always assumed that if they got injured, they just died," Sullivan explained.

As she grew older, finished high school, and entered university, Sullivan always held in the back of her mind that touch on her foot from an onion-hungry skunk. Because of Zorro, she had decided that helping animals would be her life's work, but she had not kept in touch with Swinimer, and didn't know about the internationally recognized rescue, rehabilitation, and release program those four cages in an Eastern Passage backyard had grown into.

By late 2008, Sullivan was attending Nova Scotia Agricultural College and looking for a place to get in some required volunteer hours with animals. During a web search, she typed in "wildlife" and up popped "Hope for Wildlife" and the name Hope Swinimer.

"I must have called her several times a week for at least four months. I just completely harassed her to get in there. And then I went to my first orientation, and I've been there ever since," Sullivan said. "I knew once I found her again, this was where I was supposed to be."

Sullivan was a volunteer worker that summer at Hope for Wildlife. In the spring of 2010, Swinimer, on a whim, applied for the contract to run the Halifax city pound service, and won. She opened Homeward Bound City Pound and one of the first people she hired was Tiffany Sullivan.

Surrounded by people who shared her dedication, Swinimer led the fight for provincial permission that would allow a private group to do wildlife rehabilitation in Nova Scotia. When government officials said she could not get a permit for a private rehabilitation centre because no guidelines for such a document existed, she promptly sat down with two biologists and wrote what was needed.

Now other people in Nova Scotia who care for wildlife are following in her footsteps, under regulations she helped create.

"Wildlife has been the passion of Hope Swinimer's life and she certainly has lived by that passion," said Jen Costello, a regional biologist for the Nova Scotia Department of Natural Resources.

That passion is rooted in a purpose that goes beyond Hope for Wildlife's doctoring and nurturing of injured animals. Swinimer believes most people do not know enough about the wild things they share their province with. If they can be taught to care, wildlife will be more than just roadkill or something smelly that has moved in under their garage. It will become a public treasure, as precious to everyone as it is to Hope Swinimer.

Underlying all the adventures retold here, that is the one real hope.

CHAPTER 1

AN ANIMAL
TO LEARN BY

Animals can change people. Sometimes they bring out the best in us, other times the worst. When Hope Swinimer first opened herself to working with wild creatures, she was full of love and good intentions, but also a lot of innocence. Swinimer lacked the wide diversity of experience that could come only from hands-on animal rehabilitation. These were not people's pets and there had been no private group before her in Nova Scotia licensed to do the work she intended. Swinimer was stepping into what seemed like one never-ending wildlife crisis, and would slowly learn what it took to get this demanding task right. In that, she had help from the wild world she was trying to save. One animal in particular taught her vital lessons in those early years and, in doing so, forced her to change and grow.

RIVER

Many younger workers at Hope for Wildlife only knew the otter called River by reputation. They had heard he was difficult and through innuendo understood that the way their organization handled predators could be traced to trial and error with him. If asked, senior volunteers who were around during his stay had comments that ranged from "River! I could tell you stories about him, but probably shouldn't" to "Do you want to see my scars?" to "He was a handful, but a magnificent handful."

For Hope Swinimer, River had been a watershed. Before his arrival, she had rules for handling predators, but many had only been tried on smaller animals, not on one of River's size and spirit. By the time he left Hope for Wildlife, the reality of life with an otter had forced many changes. He came just as Swinimer's work started to build momentum and was her first large predatory mammal raised to adulthood, a harbinger of what Hope for Wildlife would face as it grew to become the paramount agency in Nova Scotia wildlife rescue and rehabilitation.

Swinimer often said she learned more from River than any other wild guest. He taught her about herself, but also about animals, their intelligence, and the power of instinct. Most importantly, River taught her about the danger lurking in wild creatures, no matter how close humens think they are to them.

"He taught me just how delicate the balance is in what we do," explained Swinimer. "It can cause the life and death of both an animal and a person if you do it wrong. I learned with River just how big of a thing we are messing in when we do wildlife rehabilitation."

The story of River began on a June evening in 2000. Swinimer had just arrived home from her day job as manager of the Dartmouth Veterinary Hospital when there was a knock at her door. Outside were a man and woman she didn't know, and he was carrying a large, white plastic bucket, lid on.

"Here, take this," they said to a surprised Swinimer, extending the bucket in expectation.

Swinimer hesitated and asked what was inside. The couple replied they weren't certain, but they had been watching it for over two weeks and it couldn't keep up with the rest of its family. It couldn't move very well and kept getting left behind.

"I think they knew what it was," Swinimer said, "but they weren't a hundred per cent sure. Anyway, they just handed me the bucket and left, so there I was with this closed bucket and no idea what was inside. I remember just like it was today, slowly taking the

River as a youngster: Hope for Wildlife had never before fostered a predator this large and had no idea of the special problems that come with an adolescent male carnivore.

cover off and looking in. This face was staring up at me. It was all head, very little body, and it just looked up at me and cried. It was a baby river otter, and the most beautiful thing I ever saw. I was scared to death. I knew nothing about otters. I didn't even know what kind of otters we had in Nova Scotia."

She estimated River's age at about two months and then started frenzied research. What to feed it? Should it be on the bottle or whole food? Swinimer hit the books and Internet and then called other rehab centres across the country. Once she had enough information to care for her new animal, Swinimer got medical help. X-rays at the Eastern Shore Animal Hospital showed no structural damage, but there was evidence of soft tissue trauma around the spine. River was not using his hind legs, it appeared, because an eagle, dog, or coyote had grabbed him. He was put on medication and within six weeks was a normal young otter again.

Hope for Wildlife had never had an animal like River. He was active, playful, and intelligent, with big eyes that melted hearts. When he first arrived, he still had razor sharp baby teeth, but soon realized that humans gave food and stopped using them on his handlers. For Swinimer, he became a special project that had the ability to instill awe in everyone he met.

"It was amazing. I remember I brought him in to work one day for a checkup, and we were having a lunch meeting," Swinimer said. "All the staff was sitting in the lunch room and no one knew I had him. It went quiet, and I asked if anyone wanted to see an otter. They all stared at me and said yes, so I went running out, got him, and sat him right in the middle of the room. I've never seen anything like it. These are people who see different animals every day, but the whole room was silent. Everyone just stared at this beautiful creature. He just took your breath away."

Otters are one of nature's most interesting mammals and have been the subject of many books and several movies. In Nova Scotia, they are the largest and most aquatic of the Mustelidae, or weasel, family. They are the fastest swimmers of all four-legged animals, with a top speed of about ten kilometres an hour on the surface, six and a half under water. Their nostrils and ears close over when they submerge, allowing them to dive to depths of twenty-five metres and stay under for up to eight minutes. Otters have a membrane that covers their eyes when they dive, allowing them to see under water, almost like swim goggles, but whiskers are their most important hunting aid. They pick up the water vibrations from fish movement and steer the animal to what is making those vibrations. On land, river otters may look clumsy, but they can outrun a human.

River grew quickly, and with him grew a problem. An otter family ranges widely and a young otter is a traveller who plays, swims, hunts, sleeps, and learns the world with his mother and siblings. Like most predators, he does this for at least a full year before leaving the birth group. Swinimer knew River could never get all of that with her, but decided to give him enough freedom to at least experience some of it. Late in his first summer, when he was healed and able to travel on his own, she decided to soft release him, unaware of what she was about to let loose on her rehabilitation centre and the division it would cause in her staff.

THIS FAMILY STINKS

Otters, like all mustelids, have two large scent glands under the tail. These produce a very strong, liquid scent, called musk, used for marking territories and food caches, as well as attracting mates. Unlike its distant cousin the skunk, an otter cannot spray its scent. However, a freshly deposited otter signpost indeed has a very bad smell to it.

With a soft release, a caretaker gives the animal the option to come and go as it pleases. Its cage is left open and food provided for as long as needed, so the animal can explore the wild world until it is ready to make the jump to it full-time. In a hard release, an animal is taken to a remote site, let loose, and must fend for itself immediately. A hard release is common for herbivores. A deer doesn't need to be taught to eat. On the other hand, a predator needs to learn how to hunt, generally a two-year process. It was clear that releasing River the hard way would give him little chance of survival, especially as a pup that first summer.

"All day long, I'd open the door. He'd swim in the lake, do his thing, and hang out at the farm. It became his home. Every night he'd come in, go back into his cage, and I'd lock him up. This went on for almost a full year," explained Swinimer.

During that year, River continued to grow and passed through puppyhood to become a young, adolescent male otter. His home turned, by instinct, into his territory and he, as a young predator will do, came to think of himself as its alpha male. His attitude changed accordingly. Otters are by nature inquisitive and this, coupled with River's growing belief that everything at the Hope for Wildlife rehab centre belonged to him, led to what one veteran volunteer called "River incidents."

For example, it didn't take him long to figure out where the fish were stored.

Fill in the action for this setting: Contractor climbs barn roof to measure for shingling; adolescent male otter, who considers the man an intruder, follows him up the ladder. The stage is now set for another "River incident."

"He learned to climb the ladder, cross over the loft in the barn, jump down on the fridge, swing open the freezer, and grab his fish out," Swinimer remembered. "We had to put child locks on all the fridges and freezers. He even figured out how to turn the doorknob into my kitchen."

Before long, River came to think he could do whatever he wanted with the rehab centre's volunteers, and since the order was out not to physically stop him because it would provoke a conflict and traumatize him, he would try everything with them. This soon extended to visitors as well.

"I remember I started dating this new guy just about that time. He said he'd come to my house and cook me supper, and I thought that was great," Swinimer said. "So he came out to the farm. It was his first time there, and he was going to cook salmon for me. He had gone out and bought this whole great big salmon, brought it into my kitchen, and sat it on the counter. Well, River didn't miss that. He came out of nowhere, into the kitchen, grabbed the whole salmon, and took off outside with it. The new boyfriend just looked at me. Then he asked if I happened to have any chicken."

Swinimer knew through his first winter and second summer the young otter was becoming a problem. No food was safe. He'd go into workers' cars, grab their lunches, and bite any hand that came out to stop him, sometimes quite badly.

Ronda Brennan had been a volunteer with Swinimer's crew for as long as the rehab centre had been in Seaforth. She was nipped many times as River became more and more adult.

"After a while, he became very territorial," Brennan said. "It was all about food. He knew we were the ones that gave him food, but as time passed, he realized we were also the ones preventing him from getting it. We'd have to close the barn doors behind us so he didn't get in, and then he'd start chewing holes in the barn. You could hear him outside, trying to chew his way in. Then he started coming up through the floors. Anything to get in where he knew the food was."

By the time he was a yearling, River was not just interested in frozen food. He had his eye on animals that would normally be part of his diet at that age and he would bite Brennan if she got between him and his instincts.

"We had a goose in one of the cages, and River came up behind me and stuck his head by me into the cage," Brennan remembered. "I thought 'Oh dear!' and by mistake, just by instinct, I grabbed him by the scruff of the neck. Wow! He just swung around and grabbed me. I think I still have the scars. He was dominant and just ruled the roost. But it's funny. After he bit me, he just walked away, rolled belly-up, and wanted to play."

Volunteer Karen Damtoft was also around during River's time. She remembers that in his second summer, if he got into the barn, he'd be up on the counter where the food was prepared and make a great mess of things. He was "a little scary" by then, she said.

"He was getting very big by that point," Damtoft stated. "He always behaved himself pretty well with me. He did attack my boot once, but I always wore those big green ones. His tooth got stuck in it for a little while and he didn't like that. Then he ran away."

Everything written about raising young predators for release pointed out the folly of becoming too familiar with them. It was bad for the animal, but also risky for a human. These were not house pets. Certainly River wasn't, and forgetting that could prove painful.

OTTER COUSINS

River and sea otters are at the same time similar and very different animals. They are both mustelids and closely related, but one is a land mammal that lives in and around fresh water, the other a true sea mammal that rarely, if ever, comes ashore. The sea otter is slightly longer and much heavier than a river otter, with fully webbed, paddle-shaped feet that are useless on land. The river otter's feet are webbed, but also shaped for effective walking and running. River otters can be found across North America, sea otters in Pacific coastal waters.

River didn't have a lot of exposure to male humans. However, a man named Peter was there for the summer, volunteering with his daughter, and he assumed the type of male play bond that the otter would normally have with a brother, or a human male with his pet dog. They roughhoused on all fours, wrestling and paw slapping.

"Peter was a big guy," Damtoft remembered, "and River was big, in his late adolescent stage. They'd charge at each other. River would knock Peter over, and the two of them would literally be in an embrace, rolling on the floor. And River was noisy. You have to picture the grunts, squeals, and chattering he made playing like that. It was real otter play, but it was very intimidating even to watch. You were just holding your breath, hoping everything would be okay."

One day, it wasn't.

"They were rolling around on the floor, and when Peter came up, he had his hand covering his ear and this horrid look on his face. He said River had just bit him. It turned out River had pierced his earlobe, almost exactly where you would put an earring. Right through his earlobe with his teeth," Damtoft explained.

Otters nip for discipline and in play, and River had always done it. What happened with Peter was likely an accident, the other workers present thought, and if River had done it to a bigger otter

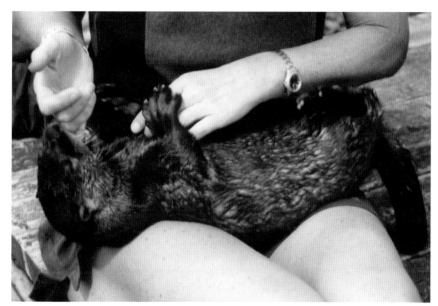

Otters are naturally playful in their first year. Most frequent forms are wrestling and play-fighting, as shown here by River. Otters sometimes play chase and, on rare occasions, toss a small live fish back and forth. All play stops as they reach adolescence.

he would have been bitten back. But Peter could not give back the discipline River would understand. Peter was usually scratched and bleeding after an otter play session and had accepted that without complaint, but once the biting reached his face, accidental or not, his relationship with River changed.

As River matured, he became less tolerant of intruders, and strangers needed to be on their guard. Swinimer remembers the time the barn roof needed repairs. She called a local contractor who came out, put up his ladder, and climbed to the peak of the very steep barn roof. Unfortunately, River had followed him up the ladder.

"River decided to grab him by the leg," Swinimer remembered. "The roofer was up there screaming at me to get the otter off him, and I was yelling back there was nothing I could do. After about twenty minutes, River came back down. The roofer left. He never gave me a quote and he never called me back."

Sleek and beautiful, otter pups such as River have been the subject of several books and movies.

The pressure of having River loose on a soft release, whether it gave him a better chance for survival or not, was creating a rift within the Hope for Wildlife volunteer staff. Swinimer knew it and was forced to reexamine what she had always thought was an honourable axiom: the animal comes first. Things were getting tense.

"Everybody at Hope for Wildlife has always got along amazingly well. There's very little gossip, very little complaining. It's just a place people come because they love it. River caused that to go a little astray. There were people who understood soft release programs and how they worked, then there was another group who thought this animal was far too dangerous to allow anywhere near the general public," said Swinimer.

Swinimer realized she had a major problem, one of her own making. She had set River loose on her property to orientate him, but at the same time, she had always put education ahead of all other aspects of her work. This meant an open door policy for visitors, and both adults and children often dropped by unannounced.

"This animal could kill a child, and had made that territory its territory. I had created a really dangerous situation," she admitted.

People arriving with food in their cars had become the source of a number of incidents.

"With any wild animal you can't argue with them, discipline them, or tell them no," said Swinimer. "So if someone pulled into the driveway, opened the car door, and he ran into the car, you didn't yank him out. You bribed him out. And if there was food in that car, you didn't grab the lunch bag from the otter, because he would nail you. This sort of thing happened, and not just once."

Swinimer and her staff came to realize that their policy of allowing the public near more passive animals did not work with juvenile predators. Children, with all their enthusiasm and noise, were particularly at risk. For example, children liked to toboggan down Swinimer's back hill in the winter. River belly-slid for hours on the same hill, instinctively knowing at the first snowfall it was something an otter would do. One day a group of young children was being especially noisy on the hill and it set River off. He bit a girl, very badly. Another instinct had told him that this was his territory.

The Hope for Wildlife team were writing the book as they went. These were mistakes they would not make again, but every day was a new lesson.

While it became more and more evident that there had to be a better way to soft release a predator, River continued to play Jekyll and Hyde. Those he didn't attack were thoroughly enthralled with him. There was an open space under Swinimer's front porch and a hole up through the deck. River liked the cool, dark earth there and often lay quietly for hours. If someone came to the door, he would stick up an inquisitive head, but never threaten that person. To these people, he remained unique and interesting. They didn't find him at all intimidating.

By mid-summer of his second year, River's exploring was taking him further and further afield, and Swinimer and her workers started to see him less often. He no longer went to his pen at night, instead preferring his spot under the deck. Some nights, he didn't return at all. Swinimer felt he was growing away from her.

River could be playful, but also very demanding. As time went by, his play-fullness could no longer hide that he was growing into a deadly aquatic predator. Adult male otters weigh up to 14 kilograms.

It was well after sunset on a late July evening. River had not shown up, and Swinimer was in bed, almost asleep, when she heard a rapid but familiar patter of feet across the deck. Her otter was back, but instead of going under the deck, he was on it. She knew something was wrong and leapt from her bed.

"I went running downstairs, opened the door, and River threw his arms around my legs and wouldn't let go. He was looking up at me and just shivering. I shone the flashlight and there was another great big otter that had chased him up there. He was huge, this other otter. I couldn't believe his size! When I shone the light on him, he didn't move. He would look at me and then he'd look at River, then at me, back and forth. It was a while before he decided to leave. I let River sleep in my porch that night. It was the only night in his life I ever allowed him to sleep inside. When I inspected him in the morning, he had huge puncture wounds, so he had experienced a really bad incident with that otter. We had to get him on antibiotics, but it was a valuable lesson for him. He got to come back, think about it, and heal."

Swinimer hoped River had learned that as a juvenile male, he was not the boss of the lake. It would be a big step towards his eventual survival in the wild. He needed to know that if a larger male showed aggression, he had to get out of there or face dire consequences. However, he had yet to learn he wasn't top male at the farm and when that finally happened a few weeks later, his time at Hope for Wildlife was over.

"That night was so sad," she admitted. "My boyfriend and River did not get along, and because men seem to think that animals need to be controlled, it was always a tug of war between the two of them. One night we were lugging groceries into the house, and River came up to Dave and tried to grab the grocery bags. Dave yelled at him, made a kicking motion, and put on a general display of loud male aggression. That was the last time I ever saw River. As much as it broke my heart, maybe it was good that Dave was aggressive with him, because he needed to be out of there."

If River survived in the wild, it would likely be because he had learned his place. As it is for adolescent males everywhere, it was foolish for a young otter to pick a fight he could not win. The rehabilitation centre had also learned lessons and when predators were taken in in the future, things would be different.

CHAPTER 2

LORDS OF THE WIND AND AIR

Diurnal raptors are winged predators who hunt by day. They are at the top of the avian food chain, swift and deadly in their flight, and probably least understood and most maligned of all birds. Native and ancient peoples revered them for their power, speed, beauty, and deadliness. In Nova Scotia, their numbers include eagles, hawks, falcons, and osprey.

MARLENE

The eagle did not hesitate. She lunged out of the release box, straight upward without touching the ground, spreading wide her newly healed wings to pulse into the air and rise quickly on a field-edge updraft. For a long while, she hung there, soaring high above an Antigonish County field and the group of people on the road below.

One was a Hope for Wildlife worker who had helped her recover. Another was the university professor who had found the injured eagle and called for help. The person with the camera on her shoulder was a documentary filmmaker who had been shooting video of the eagle for five months. Still others were area adults and children, all come on an October day to see her take the freedom she had lost the previous May.

St. Francis Xavier University's Riley Olstead had been there when the story began and was there again for its end. Olstead was certain the big female bald eagle called Marlene knew she was home.

"She must have ridden that updraft for forty minutes," Olstead said. "She was just circling, checking everything out. I like to think that she was just checking to see if any of the furniture had been moved."

It had been a May morning, cool but full of promise, when Olstead and Marlene first met. Professor Olstead slipped out of her home on the outskirts of Antigonish about 6:30 for her daily run. She and her family had been in Nova Scotia less than a year after moving from Toronto, but her original home had been British Columbia, and experience there, although she didn't know it yet, was about to save an eagle's life.

"It was a crisp early morning. No sign of weather, just a nice quiet rural day in Nova Scotia," Olstead said. "I was on the North Lakeville Road, about twenty minutes into my run, when I noticed this enormous bird standing in the middle of a field."

While someone else might have taken it as just another rural sight, instinct from Olstead's youth told her something was very wrong with this picture.

"I'm from BC and I'm quite familiar with bald eagles. This looked very strange, that there would be a bird sitting that long in a field as I approached it. As I was coming up along the road, it didn't move at all," Olstead explained. "This was very, very strange."

Olstead decided to find out what was going on. Could the bird move or not? Was there something on the ground so important that the eagle refused to leave it, even when a human approached? As she drew closer, the eagle remained motionless. Then she got her answer.

"All of a sudden, it pushed off and started doing these magnificent leaps into the air, bounding away," she related. "It was then that I saw her attempt to put out her wingspan. It was very clear that one wing was injured, probably broken."

Olstead knew the eagle wanted to take off, but could not. It was a huge, beautiful bird, she noted, but without flight would last only as long as it took another predator to find her. To make things

A flight cage was essential when Hope for Wildlife began taking care of Nova Scotia's birds of prey after the Atlantic Raptor Centre closed. Volunteers moved this one from the old centre to Seaforth.

worse, Olstead had no idea how to get help. New to the province, she was under the impression there were no resources available in rural Nova Scotia to aid one injured bird flopping about in a field. She sprinted for home, hoping her husband would have a solution. Olstead was very worried that one predator in particular would be onto the injured eagle in no time.

"I was aware of the fact that the bird was leaving a trail of downy under feathers, and that this would be picked up. Other animals would quickly become very interested, and we're pretty rich around here with coyotes," she explained.

With a very real concern that the eagle would not last long in coyote country, she burst into the house and awakened her family. Her husband, Hugh Benevides, is an environmental lawyer and he knew of Bob Bancroft, although they'd never met. However, he soon located the well-known Nova Scotian broadcaster, writer, and retired wildlife biologist and dragged him into the early morning emergency. Bancroft provided the phone number for Mark Pulsifer, regional biologist for the Nova Scotia Department of Natural Resources and one more St. FX co-worker Olstead had yet to meet. Within twenty minutes, Pulsifer was on the scene. Olstead was skeptical when she saw Pulsifer had a small portable dog kennel with him. Unaware of his years of experience, she voiced her concern that he did not understand the size of the bird involved, and got a chuckle in reply from the wildlife veteran.

DID YOU KNOW?

- The word bald comes from the Old English *balde*, meaning white.

- An eagle's eyesight is seven times better than a human's. It can see clearly for up to one and a half kilometres.

- The beak of a bald eagle is made of keratin, the same substance as human nails.

- It takes five years for a bald eagle to mature. Only adult birds have white heads and tails.

- Eagles mate for life.

- After the DDT crisis of the 1950s wiped out most of America's eagles, Nova Scotian birds were used for restocking several states.

By this time, the weather had changed and there was a steady rain as the pair tracked the feather trail across the field and into alder-thick woods. Olstead stopped at the edge of a thicket, but Pulsifer waded in, vanished, and in a short while reappeared with the bird. She was in a capture net, her talons clamped on the bar.

In the next few moments, Olstead came to realize that Pulsifer more than knew what he was doing and also received a few tips from him on handling a wild eagle. A raptor cannot be forced to release its talons once they clamp down and lock, Pulsifer told her. Instead, you make it want to let go. This Pulsifer did by throwing the net, with the eagle attached, into the air. The bird released its talons to attempt flight and was caught when it fell. Olstead noticed Pulsifer had pinned the eagle's talons with one hand and had his other on its chest. Once again, she expressed concern, this time that he was putting his hand in danger from the eagle's powerful beak. Pulsifer said not to worry. With birds of prey, it is the talons that are most dangerous, he explained. The beaks are for feeding and rarely used aggressively. Eagles are rippers, not peckers, Pulsifer said. On the other hand, if he had been holding a raven, he would never put his hand there.

As Pulsifer tucked the squawking eagle into the portable dog kennel, the container's size finally made sense to Olstead. She realized this transport cage wasn't there to make the bird comfortable; its purpose was to limit the eagle's movement so it couldn't further hurt itself. The cage would need to do that job very well. Pulsifer was facing a drive of several hours to Seaforth and the Hope for Wildlife centre, a place where this injured eagle would have a chance to stay alive.

Dr. Barry MacEachern of the Dartmouth Veterinary Hospital was used to seeing animals Hope Swinimer and her Hope for Wildlife team were trying to save. He had spent countless hours at his Tacoma Drive workplace putting to use both proven medical practice and unique experimentation to save and rebuild the lives of shattered wildlife, and his work did not stop when the animals left his hospital. Year after year, he regularly made the long journey down the Eastern Shore to Hope's site to check on his patients. He took no payment for his work. All this was done as a volunteer, because he believed in Hope for Wildlife's cause.

MacEachern's impact on injured wild creatures was vital to Hope for Wildlife, but he also did something else that had value, and certainly staying power. Whenever he worked on an animal, he gave it a name. A barred owl hit by a winter salt truck became Salty, a great horned owl delivered full of porcupine quills on Christmas Eve was naturally Eve. When a speeding car's tire crushed a pregnant wood turtle, what name would be suitable for her but Dunlop?

"I usually try to name the animals with something I will remember, to jog my memory as to either the nature of the injury or when they arrived," said MacEachern.

The new eagle from Antigonish came two days before Mother's Day. He called her Marlene, after his mother, so in the future he would remember when he first worked on her. Everyone who dealt with the bird began using the name MacEachern had tagged her with.

Riley Olstead's initial reaction that morning in an Antigonish field proved correct. Dr. MacEachern found an open fracture of the ulna, the main bone in Marlene's left wing, and it was quickly decided that if she was to have any chance of recovery the bone needed to be pinned. Even then, there was no guarantee she would fly again. An eagle's wing carries tremendous stress during flight, more per square centimetre than a large aircraft, and anything except a perfect knit would not withstand that stress.

MacEachern decided to perform a procedure called retrograde pinning. A stainless steel rod is inserted to join the two broken bone parts, and the wing is then immobilized so the pin can hold the bone in the correct position to grow together again. If the bone knitted, and everything else healed properly, the pin could be removed in about eight weeks.

The following day, Marlene was put under anaesthetic for the surgery, but an unexpected, possibly fatal, complication was discovered. Infection had worked its way into the open wound and was well established. Operating on a badly infected wound is always risky, but with a bird, problems are potentially greater. Mammals can be shaved to keep the area around the wound clean. Birds, however, have feathers, not fur. They cannot be shaved, which always presents a danger of re-infection. A quick decision was made to complete the surgery despite the new problem, and the pin was put in place, the wound closed. Loaded with antibiotics and anti-inflammatory pain control, the eagle was taken back to Hope for Wildlife to recuperate.

While Marlene was unconscious at the Dartmouth Veterinary Hospital, someone new entered her life. Shannon MacDougall was a University of Kings College journalism graduate who worked for Arcadia Entertainment in Halifax. Her company was preparing a television series on the work of Hope for Wildlife, and she joined the field unit just in time to shoot her first surgery—Marlene's. MacDougall remembered one moment that day as a life-lasting image. After it, her camera followed Marlene through all five months of recovery.

"The most vulnerable I ever saw her was in the arms of Dr. Barry as she came out from under anaesthetic at the vet hospital," she said. "He held her head in his hands and cradled her against his chest. It's something you won't often see, that's for sure."

Over the next few months, Marlene's wing slowly healed, and MacDougall was there, constantly filming. As she gradually grew familiar with Seaforth's wild guests, MacDougall came to realize each species had a signature trait. There was the comic playfulness of a young raccoon, the shy beauty of a fox kit, and the regal aloofness and desire for freedom of the hawks and eagles.

Dr. Barry MacEachern tending to a pelican, just one of the many different types of birds that make their way to Hope for Wildlife.

"Birds of prey are fascinating in that they never ever, no matter how cared for and tended to, form any attachment to their human caretakers. They remain skittish and sort of scary. I spent hours in their enclosure, waiting to capture them eating on film. Those birds would chew through your arm if it meant getting out that door and back to the wild," MacDougall said.

"It was so different from songbirds. I sat in their enclosure to get some footage of them fluttering about before Allison and Hope were scheduled to release them. One would not stop landing on my head, hand, leg, camera, or any other surface near me. It was quite charming. It seemed all the bird wanted to do was make friends and sing me a song."

Of all the birds of prey at Hope for Wildlife that summer, the fire for freedom seemed to burn hottest in Marlene. Of course, no one really knew why. Most said it was simply the natural instinct of a predator to be free. However, a few wondered if there was a nest that had been left unattended that May. Or whether a mate still looked for her. Eagles bond for life and will only take a new partner if the old one dies, and since Marlene was a full adult, at least five years old, she likely had a mate. Was she desperate to tell him she was still alive? She escaped twice in her third month, both times before success was physically possible. The first attempt came when she was still being held in a small isolation cage. No one knows how she got out. The best guess is that the cage was not properly closed. Whatever the cause, she didn't hesitate. A group of Hope for Wildlife workers enjoying a mid-summer lunch at a picnic table next to the barn suddenly realized there was an eagle standing between them and the lake, eyeing them warily.

"Oh, look at the eagle there," said Tiffany Sullivan. The others stopped eating, glanced at the bird, and then at each other. There was silence as they all fell to the same conclusion. If there was an eagle doing nothing in particular, just sitting there between barn and lake in Hope for Wildlife's backyard and giving a group of stunned workers a baleful stare, the chance was very good that it was one of theirs making a break for it. They jumped up as one and ran towards her.

As it turned out, their instincts may have been dead on, but this probably was not the best capture method. Even a bird recovering from wing surgery, unable to fly, will not sit there impassively when faced by a wave of stampeding wildlife workers. Marlene's response was to jump into the lake and Sullivan, fearing the bird would drown, followed. Luckily, this part of the lake was not very deep. Sullivan got behind Marlene and tried to keep her from reaching deeper water.

"I started waving my arms in front of the eagle so it would go the other way, rather than towards me. Thank god it worked. The bird jumped back onto dry land and went barrelling off into the bushes on the opposite side of the driveway," Sullivan said.

Hope for Wildlife raptor specialist Nicole Payne shows the capture net she tried to swim with during Marlene's second escape attempt.

With Sullivan now out of the water and blocking the drive, Sara Seemel took over. She sent another worker for a capture blanket and plunged into the mixture of thorns, weeds, and small bushes in pursuit of Marlene. The exhausted eagle resisted to the end, finally flopping onto her back, talons menacing, in the traditional last-ditch defensive display of a cornered raptor. When the blanket arrived, it was placed over her to neutralize her talons, and a tired, wet, but still furious Marlene was taken back to her cage.

X-rays showed her wing had healed, so Marlene was moved to a flight cage. There, with other birds of prey, she was supposed to relish the space, start flapping, and get her muscles ready for release. It was immediately apparent, however, that Marlene was not going to cooperate. She refused to fly. Other birds were in various stages of pre-release, beating their wings, flying, or gliding from one end of the long cage to the other. But not Marlene. If she wanted to get anywhere in the pen, she did it on the ground. Some workers thought there was still a problem with the wing, others thought that she was sulking after her first foiled escape. A few said she was lonely. Hope Swinimer had her own opinion.

"We could find no medical reason why she wasn't flying. We thought maybe she was just getting fat and lazy!" Swinimer said.

Whatever the reason, a few weeks went by and Marlene was still behaving like a wingless bird, so Dr. MacEachern was called in.

SKY HUNTERS OF THE DAYLIGHT
THE DIURNAL RAPTORS IN NOVA SCOTIA:

- Bald eagle
- Broad-winged hawk
- Cooper's hawk
- Kestrel
- Merlin
- Northern goshawk
- Northern harrier
- Osprey
- Peregrine falcon
- Red-tailed hawk
- Sharp-shinned hawk

One afternoon, he arrived with Hope for Wildlife Coordinator Allison Dube. Also present was Shannon MacDougall, still on Marlene's story and eager to film the examination.

"I wasn't sure why she wasn't flying as the bone was healed, so I figured I should take a look," MacEachern said. "We went to the far end of the flight cage to try to make her fly to the other end. Instead, she just ran to the far end on the ground. Allison and I decided to catch her so I could take a look, but when we started towards her, we noticed the door was open. Unfortunately, so did she."

With her was another running-but-not-flying eagle called Chester.

"As Dr. Barry and I went towards Marlene, she hopped up and—this is the good part—her wing hit the hook that was holding the door closed and knocked it open. She ran out. Chester sort of looked stunned for a second, like he saw us and was thinking about it, and then he also decided to go for the door," recalls Dube.

However, MacDougall saw it differently. She had been shooting when Dube and MacEachern entered the enclosure and followed them as they went through the door and up to the far end to confront Marlene. She tried to swing the door closed as she went through, camera operating, but it didn't catch. MacDougall recorded the Marlene and Chester breakout and said it would be part of the resulting video documentary.

Nicole Payne works with an injured osprey. This provincial bird of Nova Scotia is considered by Hope for Wildlife to be the most difficult raptor to work with.

"By next autumn [2010], you'll be able to watch the spectacle on OasisHD, complete with my voice peeping a muted, 'oh no'," she said.

Neither bird was flying when they burst out of the flight cage, but both were making top speed on land. Chester bolted up the hill towards the deer pen. Dube was right behind him. Marlene headed downhill, through a thick patch of thorn bushes next to the lake, with MacEachern giving chase.

Meanwhile, Nicole Payne and Laura Bond were working in Dan's Den, one of the raccoon enclosures, when they heard shouts for help from the direction of the flight cage. Bond headed up the hill to aid Dube. Payne went to MacEachern's assistance near the lake. She found him with a net, bogged down in the thorns, saw Marlene on land next to the water, and made a beeline for her.

"Marlene had settled near the lake, but not in the water," MacEachern remembered. "Then Nicole came running from the other direction straight towards her. Marlene jumped into the lake! Nicole then followed suit and jumped in to get her! I wasn't sure how Nicole planned to swim, carry a large net, and catch the eagle, but she was determined!"

The steely gaze of a bald eagle. "Those birds would chew through your arm if it meant getting out that door," said videographer Shannon MacDougall of Arcadia Entertainment.

Payne was known for her work with raptors. They were her first love and she had already begun training for accreditation as a falconer, so MacEachern assumed the situation at the lake was under control and headed back to help catch Chester.

The situation was not under control. The water was much deeper than where Marlene had ditched the first time. Payne had to swim more often than wade and quickly found she could not carry the capture net, so she discarded it. The bird kept moving, but could not lift itself out of the water, and while her feathers gave temporary buoyancy, an eagle's plumage is not waterproofed like a duck's. Payne called for a blanket so she could make a hand capture and someone threw her one, but as soon as it hit the lake surface, Payne realized another problem. It immediately absorbed water until moving it was like carrying a massive stone. But she pulled the blanket with her and eventually caught up to Marlene.

Somehow, she got the sodden cloth around the bird, pinned its talons, and struggled to shore. Her wet clothes, the blanket, and the soggy eagle became an almost impossible burden when she tried to climb out. With help, she finally made it up the bank, then crashed alone through the thorn bushes straight to the flight cage, dumped the bird inside, and collapsed from exhaustion. Chester was already back in custody.

A short time later, MacEachern examined Marlene's wing and found nothing structurally wrong with it. She was just not in shape to fly, and he told Hope's staff to put her on a physical training program. This consisted of volunteers chasing her up and down the flight cage whenever they fed her. One of those involved in this was Payne.

"Each day, we would get her flying from one end of the flight cage to the other, making notes of how she was progressing. At first, she would hop from end to end while flapping her wings. Eventually, she was starting to get lift and flying further and further. When she was finally ready for release, she was flying around obstacles really well and taking off and landing with excellent control," she said.

On October 17, 2009, it was Nicole Payne who drove the cardboard carton containing Marlene to Antigonish. Videographer Shannon MacDougall was there to record the end of the adventure. Riley Olstead, her family, and several neighbours came out to North Lakeville Road to view the release.

"It was one of the most beautiful releases I've ever seen," Payne said. "She got up over the trees and just started soaring, higher and higher. She went up hundreds of feet, just enjoying the ability to fly again. She was home."

As the humans below smiled, shook hands, and prepared to go with Olstead for a meal of celebration, someone noticed a change above them. Now just a speck of black against a grey October sky, Marlene was still circling, but not alone. Another bird had joined the dance, gliding with her in the slow, soaring gyre of an eagle pair.

It was, said Payne, as if someone had been waiting for her.

CHAPTER 3

SOMETIMES, IT DOESN'T WORK

Hope for Wildlife receives damaged goods. No bird or beast comes to them when nothing is wrong. Some have physical damages so severe that not even the most wishful thinking can imagine them well again. Others have only bumps and bruises that a few quiet days will cure. Most tread a line somewhere in between, with the outcome never completely certain. The same is true of emotional damage, though in that realm, nothing shows up in an x-ray or blood test. What makes both types of trauma so different from human ailments is that we can tell the doctor what we feel. They cannot. A lot of work and an equal amount of heartbreak can result.

PRISSY

The three R's of Hope for Wildlife are Rescue, Rehabilitation, and Release. When things go well, a wild creature moves smoothly from one step to the next, towards freedom. However, there is a problem that can rear its head anywhere in the process. It is called imprinting.

Simply put, imprinting is when a wild creature identifies a human as its natural companion or life model. The animal loses or never develops its natural

When Hope for Wildlife began caring for injured and orphaned fawns in 2007, this was their first patient. He was called Reid.

fear of people and often does not identify with its own kind. Cute and cuddly young orphans, especially raccoons and deer, attract humans whose instinct is to nurture them as they would a child. If imprinting results, the chance for a successful release back to the wild is lost.

Hope for Wildlife saw imprinting's tragedy begin to unfold in 2007, their first year doing deer rehabilitation. Despite best intentions, a young buck was doomed even before he arrived at the centre.

That spring, Hope Swinimer's life was in shambles. She had just been diagnosed with cancer and broken up with her boyfriend of seven years. Her dream to rehabilitate white-tailed deer had finally come true, but on very short notice, giving Swinimer only four months to prepare a deer-safe enclosure and train her staff for a new animal. This left her more exhausted than usual, but buoyed by the knowledge that she would become caretaker for orphaned fawns in Nova Scotia that year.

During the previous winter, the Government of Canada had told Nova Scotia that the Shubenacadie Wildlife Park could no longer collect and foster orphaned fawns. There was a fear that bringing wild deer into the park's captive herd might transmit chronic wasting disease, which was on the rise. Hope for Wildlife applied for and took over the job, even though it meant a lot of hurried preparations for an already overtaxed Swinimer.

"I couldn't believe it! I was so excited!" she said. "I'd only been asking for about five years. I started building the enclosure. It took me four months and forty thousand dollars. It's over a half acre, eight feet tall, and well constructed. There's a barn too, with hot water, everything you would need. There's a morgue up there. Everything had to be separate from the main rehab, mainly because of chronic wasting disease and those worries."

When the call came to collect their first fawn, a male they would call Prissy, it was Swinimer herself who answered. The circumstances sounded unusual from the beginning.

"Prissy was a problem from the day he came to us," Swinimer said, "and that was strange, because we didn't think he would be. We got a call from Truro saying they'd had a fawn there for over a month. They had been hand-raising it, but now they were moving away to England, so they needed someone to come get it. I sent two of my inexperienced volunteers to pick up what I thought would be an extremely tame fawn."

CHRONIC WASTING DISEASE (CWD)

CWD is a fatal degenerative brain disease similar to mad cow disease. There is no evidence it can affect people or domestic livestock. In Canada, the vulnerable animals are white-tailed deer, mule deer, moose, elk, and woodland caribou. It has not yet been a problem in Nova Scotia.

A fawn bottle rack, one way Hope for Wildlife keeps young deer from imprinting on humans.

The workers drove to the address given on the phone, but immediately felt there had been a mistake. It was a mansion. The door was answered by a maid and opened to reveal marble floors and a spiral staircase. Almost apologetically, they asked if there was a deer to be picked up, completely convinced they had the wrong place, and were astounded a moment later when a two-month-old fawn entered the lobby.

"It just came walking out. Not only had it been in the house, it had been raised in the house," said Swinimer.

The would-be rescuers quickly discovered the deer was quite happy right where he was and didn't want to leave his mansion. They wrestled him into the van, but he went berserk, throwing himself at the walls, crashing head against metal. One worker had to sit on him all the way to Seaforth. It was something people who work with wildlife hate to do, but it probably saved Prissy's life.

At the Hope for Wildlife shelter, things did not improve.

"He started running as soon as we put him in the pen, and he didn't stop running for the rest of his time with us. He was the wildest deer I've ever seen," said Swinimer.

Contact with fawns is minimized at the shelter to prevent imprinting. The fawns are monitored on a video system and bottle fed from a rack inserted into the pen, not by hand. Prissy was not old enough to be off the bottle, but he refused to feed with the other young deer. Only once or twice per week, Swinimer said, did he take food this way.

Although he grew in his time with Swinimer into an impressive, well-developed young buck, Prissy neither lost his wildness nor behaved like the other deer. Finally, after the close of hunting season in late autumn, it came time to put that year's fawns back into the wild, and for Prissy this proved a disaster. It was the first deer release by Hope for Wildlife, and the Department of Natural Resources wanted all the animals ear tagged before they were let go. Swinimer predicted that Prissy would not cooperate, and she was correct. He was too quick to be caught, and too evasive to be hit with a tranquilizer dart, no matter how hard or long Department of Natural Resources staff tried.

"They had Prissy so crazy, he smashed up against the fence in three places, did something to his jaw, and broke one of his antler buds. By the time the other deer were ready to go, he was a mess. We still had no ear tag in him, and he was bleeding. Just a mess," said Swinimer.

Every attempt to load Prissy with the others failed. He was too wild, uncontrollable, to get into the trailer. However, Swinimer made up her mind that he deserved freedom and decided that once the other deer were gone, she would leave the pen door open. A free Prissy could roam the woodlands adjacent to her Seaforth property and not be alone. Wild deer came out nightly to graze on the margins of her land.

Prissy didn't take long to find the open doorway and bolt through it. That, thought the Hope for Wildlife workers, was that. The deer had gone back to where he belonged and was out of their lives forever.

They were wrong. It turned out that in all the time he was with them, Hope for Wildlife had misjudged what was bothering this deer. Prissy had wanted to be free, but not in the wilderness. He wanted the freedom to be with people, friendly ones who would make a fuss over him, feed him treats, and pet him as they had in Truro.

THE DEER FAMILY

There are five members of the deer family found in North America. These are moose, American elk, caribou, mule deer, and white-tailed deer. Moose are the largest deer species in the world, American elk (Wapiti) the second largest.

Swinimer was astounded. Because of his wild behaviour, she had missed that he had imprinted during his month in a mansion. Swinimer had hoped the deer would head into the woods and live a normal life when she released him, but this little buck had other ideas. He knew where the handouts were.

"What does Prissy do? He makes friends with everybody in the community," Swinimer sighed. "Walks right up to people. Lets children get on his back, put their book bags on him. Goes to bus stops. He became a different animal when he was free, but we knew it was Prissy because he had this droopy face and the broken antler. He was becoming a real concern to our community. What could I do? I would never have let him go in my backyard if I didn't think he was the wildest deer I'd ever seen."

Prissy tried for eight months to get the people of Seaforth to make him their pet, and Swinimer kept hoping he would hear the call of the wild. Neither happened. It was late August 2008 and Prissy was now an impressive spike-horned yearling. Swinimer didn't want Hope for Wildlife's reputation sullied by one oddball deer. She was also worried children might be injured because of her mistake, and she knew, as well, that come hunting season, Prissy would be the first animal shot, probably while he was begging for treats. The decision was made to recapture him and transport him to a hard release spot far from Seaforth.

Several attempts to hit him with a tranquilizer dart accomplished nothing. Once, when a dart struck him, he ran off seemingly unaffected and Hope for Wildlife workers combed the nearby woods and fields for hours, attempting to find what they were

By autumn, a spring fawn has lost its childhood spots and is ready for release. Its new coat is the brownish grey of dead grass and leaves.

certain was a downed deer. They worked until after midnight but found nothing and the next morning he was back at his usual school bus stop, unaffected.

Prissy was still a regular visitor to the rehabilitation cages at Swinimer's place, but couldn't be lured into a pen. Finally, one of the male volunteers decided enough was enough. He would bull-dog Prissy like a rodeo steer and drag him into a cage, whether he wanted it or not. This was not a good idea.

The worker made a lunge for Prissy and managed to grab his antlers. However, it quickly became obvious that this was no longer the weak little fawn of the previous summer.

"All I could see was his legs flying as Prissy threw him back and forth," said Swinimer. "He was afraid to let go because the deer was angry enough to butt him."

The man finally escaped, his hands bleeding and a bit bruised. Fortunately, Prissy had neither gored nor kicked him when he let go.

Meet Prissy the Problem. Shown here in his second summer, the damage he did to his antlers and face resisting release the previous year is obvious.

"Well, that didn't turn out like I thought it would," he said to Swinimer.

In the end, consistent effort paid off and they were able to tranquilize and recapture the deer. Workers placed Prissy's unconscious form into the trailer used for releases, and with him, John, another late-release deer. If Prissy had been conscious, Swinimer would have feared for John's life, but the yearling buck was out cold, so she decided to make a run to a wildlife preserve far down the Eastern Shore where both animals could be safe from hunters during the upcoming season. Near Ecum Secum, Swinimer heard what sounded like World War Three breaking out in the trailer. She stopped and went back to the trailer, hoping it wasn't what she feared. But it was. Prissy had woken up.

"I couldn't get any more tranquilizers into him, he was smashing himself silly, and I knew he was going to kill himself," said Swinimer. "He was stomping all over John and we had to get him out of there or he'd kill both of them. There was only one thing to do. I opened the doors and let him go."

A few months passed. Swinimer was again certain she had seen the last of Prissy, but suddenly it was November, on the eve of hunting season, and the local news media was full of reports of a young, one-antlered buck that had befriended the good people of Ecum Secum. Everyone was giving him handouts. Children loved him. The Department of Natural Resources had been called in because nobody wanted to see this friendly animal shot. People in Ecum Secum even had a name for him. They called him Bucky.

Back in Seaforth, Swinimer and her staff watched the television news with apprehension. The Ecum Secum deer looked suspiciously familiar, and it didn't take long to confirm it: Prissy had become Bucky. While Hope for Wildlife tried to decide what, if anything, would be gained by sharing what they knew about the history of this animal, the Nova Scotia Department of Natural Resources came to the rescue. They assured Ecum Secum that its favourite deer would be safe and un-shot in the Shubenacadie Wildlife Park. There he could have a pen and a life of ease surrounded by young female deer.

Hope Swinimer and her workers decided the matter was out of their hands and said nothing, although they did wonder whether the Natural Resources vehicle made it from Ecum Secum to Shubenacadie in one piece. It was several months before they heard the final chapter of a life ruined by imprinting.

In the end, Prissy was unchanged except for his name. He was as wild and crazy when caged with other deer at the Shubenacadie Wildlife Park as he had been with Hope for Wildlife. The Department of Natural Resources could do nothing with him or for him and finally decided to put him down.

Prissy had lived his entire life not knowing he was a deer. He had been conditioned to think he was a household pet, and that was something that could not be undone. The little fawn that had crossed a marble floor towards what should have been freedom, in reality never had a chance.

CHAPTER 4

THE PINE MARTEN REPORT

As our world changes, so do the things that live in it, and that applies to humans and animals alike. If a person from two hundred years ago visited Nova Scotia today, they would find it difficult to recognize the place and would soon realize that many of the birds and animals they were once familiar with are either very scarce or no longer here. The caribou are gone. Moose, lynx, and pine marten barely hang on, teetering on the brink of extinction in the province. The last bastion for all three is the Cape Breton Highlands. There are many theories on why such animals are gone or leaving, and opinions on how to bring them back are just as abundant, each supported or denied by a multitude of experts. Every once in a while, someone asks why these experts can't just stop arguing and do something. It usually gets him or her into trouble. Hope Swinimer has, occasionally, been in that position.

GRETEL

One of the things Swinimer had to learn as she established herself in wildlife rehabilitation was how to do the dance of propriety. The Department of Natural

Resources, with the full weight of regulations behind it, was her partner in this great wildlife waltz, and she was expected to dutifully follow its lead.

It was always a tentative two-step. Swinimer heeded regulations begrudgingly and was always very ready to skewer them the moment she thought animal interests were at stake. Her willingness to fling herself in front of legal bulldozers on behalf of wildlife inspired media attention and growing public awe. Facing off with her on a legal issue had all the pleasantries of mugging the people's guardian angel of creatures wild. Rightly or wrongly, the public saw her with wings and a halo.

In 2002, the bob, weave, and jab that had been Hope for Wildlife's dancing match with the Department of Natural Resources since Swinimer took in her first animal finally came to a crescendo. She found herself backed into a corner over a young pine marten named Gretel. Swinimer decided to fight.

"Gretel," she said, "was a hill I was willing to die on."

A marten is a member of the Mustelidae or weasel family, in size bigger than the mink but smaller than the fisher. Like all mustelids, it has anal glands that can make a stink, but nothing as bad as its cousin the skunk. Martens are creatures of mature and old growth coniferous forest. There isn't much of that left in Nova Scotia, so there aren't many of these animals left either. A marten is a carnivore, both a treetop and a ground-level hunter, and its traditional prey is the red squirrel.

The Gretel crisis did not initially involve Hope for Wildlife. It was rooted in a 1980s decision by the Nova Scotia Agricultural College in Truro. Pine marten were endangered on mainland Nova Scotia, with a small remnant still hanging on precariously in the highlands of Cape Breton, so the college decided to start a breed-and-release program to repopulate the mainland, using marten from New Brunswick. They were extremely successful in the first two years, but then the Department

NOT AQUATIC

Unlike their cousins the mink and otter, pine marten have distaste for water and seldom swim. However, they are reported to swim well if forced to.

This small animal almost caused Hope Swinimer's arrest when she fought government regulations to keep her. "Gretel was a hill I was willing to die on," Swinimer said.

of Natural Resources found out and ordered them to stop. There had been no study done to determine if pine marten from northern New Brunswick were genetically the same as those few left in Nova Scotia, and without that study, introductions were illegal. The Agricultural College, with a lot of animals and an active breeding program, changed what it was doing and started fur farming instead.

Enter Hope Swinimer. She believed children in Nova Scotia were learning about endangered animals from all over the world but not those in their home province. Swinimer asked Natural Resources for permission to get a marten for use in education, to show Nova Scotians a native species they had likely never seen, and probably would never see in the wild. For four years, the Department denied this request.

There were three reasons why officials at DNR were said to oppose Swinimer's request. One was that she was a rehabilitation centre operator and pine marten were not on her rehab license. Secondly, Nova Scotians could already see marten in a display

Like all Mustelidae, the pine marten Gretel could be cute one minute, a darting little demon the next.

pen at the Shubenacadie Wildlife Park. And, of course, there was a third small issue that had been raised before: Swinimer was not supposed to be doing educational work. That was the job of Natural Resources.

Swinimer seldom took no for an answer on such matters, and each year she was denied, she became more adamant.

"I really felt that Nova Scotians needed to know what was going on right in their own backyards, and what better way than to have an endangered species from Nova Scotia for them to learn about?" she said. "DNR said no four years in a row, but I'm very persistent. I just pick, pick, pick away until I hopefully get the answer I want."

MARTEN HUNTERS

"Curious," "quick," and "ferocious" are the best words to describe a pine marten on the hunt. Although known as excellent climbers, they take most of their food on the ground with the exception of birds' eggs and nestlings. Marten endlessly and inquisitively search the roots of downed trees, under stumps, in hollow trees and logs, and through young growth coniferous thickets. In winter, they often hunt under the snow, following squirrel tunnels. Loggers have reported seeing them stealing human food left unguarded.

Then one day, fate stepped it up a notch. The Agricultural College called to tell Swinimer one of their female marten had died shortly after giving birth. There were two little ones, eyes still closed, and could she save them? Would she come to get them? Swinimer did not have the required permit but she was in Truro within an hour to take the babies.

The pair were named Hansel and Gretel, and both were ill, the male very ill. He died only a few days after arriving in Seaforth and from his necropsy the cause was found to be a parasite passed on from his mother. It was easily treated once identified, but Gretel was already in bad shape and it took around-the-clock care to save her.

Swinimer knew from the outset that Gretel would never be released. The Department of Natural Resources had stopped the College release program and would be watching her. Instead, she took the young marten into her home, gave it special care, scrapped all rehabilitation training, and began to raise Gretel to be friendly and comfortable with people so she could one day serve in education. For about four months, no one seemed to notice what Swinimer was doing. Then one day, it turned out she had been watched all along.

"Out of the blue I got a letter from the Department of Natural Resources saying what I was doing was illegal. I had to give up

In her lush winter coat, Gretel shows her friendly side to a young guest.

Gretel. I was not allowed to keep her and that if I didn't turn her over, they would put out a warrant for my arrest," Swinimer said.

The threat of arrest was based on the fact that no one in Nova Scotia was allowed to keep wildlife as pets, and since this animal was not being rehabbed for release, it was a pet. That was the Department of Natural Resources' interpretation of the law. But it was not Hope Swinimer's. She was aware of the regulation, but did not consider Gretel a pet, just as she had not considered other rescued animals that needed special care pets.

While Department of Natural Resources brass threatened its founder and director, Hope for Wildlife still received orphans and injured daily from Natural Resources field workers, and Swinimer and her volunteers treated the animals brought to them with care they could not get elsewhere. They neither complained about numbers nor questioned their condition. Unofficially, the Hope for Wildlife staff had grown through several years of joint work to think of itself as DNR's partner in wildlife.

"I was very aware of the rules about wildlife as pets," Swinimer said. "But I didn't consider myself an ordinary citizen in wildlife matters. They were bringing me animals every day. I'd had training and was doing, I thought, a tremendous service to the province."

The resulting war of threats and words lasted a year and a half. Barry Sabean, director of Wildlife for Nova Scotia, led the attack on what Swinimer was doing with Gretel.

"The department does not support the keeping of wildlife as pets or to take such animals to schools, meetings, seminars, or any other public gathering," wrote Sabean. "People sometimes get the wrong idea and feel that it would be neat to have, say, a pet marten because they are cute and cuddly-looking."

He also pointed out that his staff had been telling Swinimer for four years she could not have a marten.

Swinimer came to believe that while the provincial wildlife workers on the front line valued what she did, the suits in offices didn't even understand it. The more they pushed her, the more she pushed back.

"I'm the kind of person who picks her battles very carefully," she said, "and I pick very few. I find I can always work things out with people, even if I have to try ten thousand times. I don't give up easily. But every once in a while, there are things you really have to take a stand on. I can probably count on one hand the number of things in my lifetime I felt strongly enough about to fight. Gretel was one of them.

"I felt that they were wrong on this, for the best interest of the animal and the province. Because of what I wanted to use Gretel for, and what her quality of life would be like, I could think of no good reason why they should say no."

To the news media, it was an irresistible story: the little wildlife worker offering her heart, the big bad government department unable to take it because of regulations, and in the middle, a cute animal. As it dragged on, more and more people came out to Seaforth to look at the creature responsible. Gretel became a celebrity and a cause.

"It was simply amazing how much publicity it got. All the politicians knew who Gretel was. I'd meet one somewhere and the first thing they'd say would be 'How's Gretel?' I was getting more and more people on my side. Politicians would come to visit, to see

Gretel and find out what all the buzz was about. They couldn't understand why I was getting so much grief and running up against so many stone walls."

In the end, the stone walls crumbled. Threatened with imminent arrest, Swinimer went for and got national media coverage, and immediately afterward two lawyers publicly offered to defend Hope and Gretel free of charge, and begged for a court date. Across Canada, network television, radio shows, newspapers, and magazines eagerly awaited Swinimer's arrest and Gretel's seizure, but suddenly and unexpectedly, it was over. A one-year permit appeared under Sabean's signature allowing Swinimer to keep Gretel for educational purposes. Every year since, another has followed, even after Director Sabean retired.

Gretel settled in, safe and legal at last, and Swinimer began trying to build a bond with her. She knew it would not be as easy with a marten as it had been with other species. Members of the weasel family can be fickle in their choice of friends, and they also can be unpredictable. Swinimer acknowledged that a relationship with Gretel was not easily forged.

"Once you get to know Gretel, she's very friendly," she explained, "but not a lot of people have bonded with Gretel. Only about five of my volunteers get along with her, play with her, interact with her. Most of them just couldn't care less about her in a lot of ways, because she wouldn't allow them to get to know her. You have to put your time and effort in with Gretel. Then she'll become your friend and she'll trust you."

Gretel, Swinimer admitted, was always a sneak…and a very intelligent one. At times, it was obvious from the look on her face she was planning something.

"She's been just like a child in her behaviour. She'll wait until you leave the room to do something bad, and she knows it's something bad, so as soon as you come back and catch her, she'll run away," Swinimer said.

Guests were her special victims and seldom escaped her curiosity.

"When people came to visit, she'd run into their pockets and grab whatever looked interesting, their cigarettes or their car keys usually. She was always in trouble, always looking for something to play with, to have fun with."

MUSTELID FAMILY PLANNING

Most female members of the weasel family can control their pregnancies until conditions are best for their offspring. Fertilized eggs are held undeveloped for several months until the mother's body tells her food and climate conditions are at their best. When her reproductive system gets the signal, the eggs develop and the young are born. This is called delayed implantation.

Gretel's playfulness may get her into trouble, but it is also the key to recapturing her when she gets outside. Swinimer reported her escapes are quite common, "maybe fifteen or twenty times all told," but never a real problem.

"I go outside near where she is, and I lay down on the grass," Swinimer explained. "She just can't resist it. She has to come over and jump on me and play. It works every time."

The playful side of Gretel has been experienced by a choice few. Many people never get past a rough introduction, and then simply avoid her. One unfortunate person, however, always gets the nasty treatment and cannot avoid it. For Swinimer's companion, Reid Patterson, it has made for many trying situations.

"She just hates him," Swinimer laughed. "It's just bizarre. She'll tolerate him if I'm there, but if he walks by and I'm not in the room, she'll lunge at him, growl, and bite him."

Swinimer believed jealousy was part of the problem, but thought it went further than that. In her mind, some men do not relate well to animals because they feel a need to control them.

"The real reason is that Reid always tried to discipline her. It's this male gene thing," Swinimer explained. "Men think they can control wildlife, and they can't. But they try, so when Gretel would do something bad, he would pound his feet and yell at her. He just set himself up for failure. Now she treats him like the enemy."

A coat like Gretel's is one reason pine marten were so popular with trappers and became rare in Nova Scotia.

Allison Dube, coordinator of Hope for Wildlife, has seen both nasty and nice sides of the pine marten and developed a theory that the two didn't depend so much on how you approach her, but when. According to Dube, it should never be forgotten that pine marten are nocturnal animals. At night, they are active, playful, and friendly. By day, they are cantankerous and just want to be left alone. With Gretel, the problem is that most people attempt to make friends with her during the daytime.

Dube remembered the first evening she met Gretel.

"She jumped around and crawled all over me," Dube said, "through the pouch of my hoodie, up my shirt, into my hood, and then hopped to the counter with blazing speed. I couldn't get enough of her. When she was still enough, I got to pat her for a second, and she was off again."

It was only later that Dube realized what had just happened.

"I was one of the lucky ones," she said. "First impressions, like with people, are so important with animals. My first experience with Gretel was as a playful, fun critter. Others aren't so fortunate. They meet her in the daytime when she growls, bites, and prefers to be left alone."

Dube knew she would never be as close to Gretel as Swinimer. However, by learning how to consider the time of day and her habits, she has come closer to the marten than other Hope for Wildlife workers, especially new recruits.

"People who meet Gretel for the first time in her 'unhappy' mood look at me like I have three heads when I tell them there are times she will crawl all over me, and I can play and wrestle with her," she said. "I'm one of the lucky ones to know Gretel the way I do."

When this book was written, Gretel was eight years old and still with Hope for Wildlife. She was cantankerous and mischievous, not mellowing at all as she slipped past middle age, but had become a respected elder in the Hope for Wildlife animal world, one who helped shape Hope Swinimer. Gretel's unsettled early days and the battle over priorities with government officials had proved an invaluable education.

"This whole thing taught me so much about government, that things often don't make sense, and that's a tough lesson to learn," Swinimer said. "It also made me wonder about education. Most people don't even know what she is. All the kids know that pandas are endangered, that certain whales are endangered. They know about rhinos, they know about things all over the world, but they do not know what is endangered right in their own backyard. I think that's a shame."

CHAPTER 5

THE MYSTERIOUS CASE OF THE MASKED ARTIST

There are those who would tell you that when Brittany the elephant slaps her trunk across a canvas at the Milwaukee County Zoo, what she creates is not art. For them, the fact that the Zoo gift shop sold thirty-six of her creations at $30 each and that people have them hanging in their homes and offices does not change a thing. It is still not art, nor is similar work done around the world by kangaroos, chimpanzees, pandas, sea lions, Komodo dragons, and orangutans. Real artists have names like Cezanne, Wyeth, Renoir, Warhol, and Picasso and are covered in glory. They are not covered in fur and called Archie, Bella, and Congo. Human art is creative and valuable; animal art is a joke worth only an amused chuckle now and then. Don't compare the two, seriously. Please, please do not compare them. Otherwise, you might find out that in 2005 at a London art auction, a painting by Congo the Chimp sold for $26,352, while ones by Warhol and Renoir went unsold.

KRAMER

One day, perhaps soon, someone will write a major academic comparison of the two master painters Claude Monet and Kramer. Each broke new ground with their creative styles, shocked the public, gained media atten-

FOOD WASHER?

The raccoon's scientific name, *Procyon lotor,* perpetuates the myth that this animal washes its food. The Latin word *lotor* means "washer." If near water, a raccoon will seem to wash its food, but scientists now believe it is reenacting an ancient species's feeding pattern, called a vacuum behaviour. Raccoons are thought to have lived originally near brooks and ponds, finding most of their food in them. Although they have adapted to live in almost any habitat, their instinct is to act as if all food comes from water, which makes them appear to be washing it.

tion, and attracted imitators who turned their personal innovations into successful new artistic movements. On that day, it will be noted that each did so despite significant visual impairment.

The major difference between Monet and Kramer was that the former gradually lost his sight, while the latter eventually gained hers. Of course, one was male and the other female, which could be worth at least some scholarly ventilation. There was also the fact that while Monet was a Frenchman, Kramer was a raccoon.

Of course, Kramer was also an orphan. That is how most raccoons arrive at Hope for Wildlife. Every spring, newborns flood the society's Seaforth rehabilitation centre in numbers so great that they regularly take up at least half of the spaces available for summer care. The rehab centre has sometimes had more than three hundred motherless kits to assess, feed, and clean up after, and it seems to get worse every year. The reason is the highly adaptable nature of a raccoon. They are no longer animals found only in the countryside. Cities and towns have increasingly become their habitat, and they are quite happy to forage through garbage bins rather than woods and meadows. Raccoons are destructive with a natural inclination for mess creation. They cannot help it. As foragers, they sort through things, and create human enemies along the way.

Raccoon orphans like Kramer and her kin are the annual result. When she comes out of a winter den, a female raccoon is lean, hungry, and ready to breed. Once she has, she finds a warm, dry place to have her litter. When raccoons were solely country animals, this place was usually a log or hollow tree. Now that they are citified, it is more likely to be an attic or under a garage. Then she goes into provider mode, and nearby available garbage is easier food than hunting can bring, and a lot quicker. Property owners see the foraging mom, get a glimpse of her entering and exiting a den, and want her gone. The female raccoon is simply trying to feed her young, but her persistence usually gets her shot or trapped. People are advised every year to check for young ones before spring elimination of a mature raccoon, but they seldom do. The adult is what they see, so that is what they get rid of. Only later do they find the starving kits. If they can still be saved and someone cares enough, in Nova Scotia they end up at Hope for Wildlife.

When the 2007 orphan raccoon deluge started, no one realized at first that the little squawker with the wiry mop of unruly hair was blind. She had quickly been named Kramer after the television character with similarly bad hair, but with so many kits tumbling, fighting, getting into things, and another lot showing up each day, it took a while to notice that Kramer would bump into things when startled, or walk straight to the end of a table and fall off. Workers began to suspect visual impairment. It appeared that Kramer knew if something near her moved, but was not sure when, how, or what.

"If you waved your hand in front of her, there would be a delayed response," said staff member Laura Bond. "If you played with toys, she would react after the toy went by, as if she was reacting to the shadow. When the vet came out to take a look at her, he could see her eyes were quite cloudy. It wasn't like cataracts, it was just that her eyes weren't clear."

Another worker who provided care for Kramer was Sara Seemel. Since the little animal had no way of knowing she was handicapped, Seemel could see no sign that it affected her personality.

"It didn't really seem to faze her at all. She was a little bit quirky, walking off things, and she did get spooked sometimes, but she got along just fine with the other raccoons. They wrestled and tussled and chewed on each other and slept in a big pile. She'd fit right in. It took us a while to figure out she was definitely impaired," she explained.

It wasn't the first time a blind raccoon had arrived at Hope for Wildlife. Raccoons are born blind, with eyes closed for several weeks, and when they open, there can be problems. Sometimes after a few months, their sight improves. Often the animal remains blind, and since after a month or so Kramer did not appear to have improved vision, the assumption was made that she was one of the unlucky ones. Kramer was removed from the "hands off" list of animals destined to be released and the staff started conditioning her to get along with humans so she might be used someday in education.

"That decision had to be made because we didn't want to release her into the wild and have something happen to her," said Bond.

The raccoon's blindness had already singled her out for special attention, but now that all contact restraints were off, Kramer became the pet of the barn and everyone's favourite. Before long, staffers were looking at what had been done for years with Sweet Pea, their three-legged house fox. Every year, orphaned fox kits were handed over to her for a good dose of vixen discipline and introduction to foxy ways.

"We thought Kramer could be like a surrogate mum to our kits when they came in. We could put them with her and she could teach them how to be raccoons," said Bond.

Kramer became spoiled. Because she appeared headed for a life full of people, she received star treatment and total coddling.

"We knew that if we were going to keep her as an educational animal, we had to try to keep her tame," said Bond. "We needed to condition her so she wouldn't be vicious to people going into the unit, so we had a special little blue harness for her and we'd take her out wherever we went. There's a corner store just two minutes down the road from Hope's and Sara and I, if we had a little break around suppertime, would put Kramer on a leash and just walk into the store with her on our shoulders. She was spoiled rotten."

It was Nicole Payne who introduced Kramer to paints. Neither she nor anyone else at Hope for Wildlife had the slightest notion of what they were about to start.

"I didn't take it seriously at all," Payne recalled. "A volunteer came out of the raccoon enclosure, Dan's Den, with muddy paw prints all up and down her khaki pant legs. She made a joke about the raccoons fingerpainting her pants again, and the idea blossomed from there."

Raccoons have paws that are twenty times more sensitive than human hands. They love to touch and handle things, appearing to seek out and relish new tactile sensations. As a blind raccoon,

Kramer, the blind raccoon who started an art movement.

Kramer's sense of touch seemed to increase in proportion to her dependence on it, which gave Payne an idea. If human children loved to spend hours feeling and smearing fingerpaints, would not a raccoon, with a tactile sense so much greater, revel in that activity even more? She started her experiment with Kramer, and it was an absolute hit. Soon other workers were involved and every raccoon was given at least one session of fingerpaint therapy.

"We thought it was a great idea. It was the perfect way of interacting with animals and having fun with them," said Bond. "When we tried with some of the raccoons, they were clearly not interested, so we'd just go with ones like Kramer who really seemed to enjoy it."

Using non-toxic, washable fingerpaints, the artistic moments happened in a large stainless steel tub. Globs of different coloured paint were placed in the bottom, then a raccoon gently deposited next to them. Usually, the raccoon would immediately start handling the paint. If they didn't, a worker would dab one paw to let them feel it. Once they started playing, a mounted blank canvas would be set beside them. Paw prints and other marks soon covered it as the raccoon explored. Often, what resulted was a complete mess, artistic gibberish, as the masked artists used not only paws but also tails and backsides to smear everything together. However, certain raccoons seemed to have a knack for creating something with form and order. Kramer was by the far the most talented, with apprentices Berrie and Tiny Tim quickly following. Sometimes, a worker would prop up a canvas and guide a paint-covered paw over it to get things started. Then the raccoon would "do the rest on their own creative design," as Bond put it.

Artist at work! This was the first of many paintings Kramer has done at Hope for Wildlife.

"They seemed to enjoy feeling it in the pads of their paws. The paint was only a sensation to them, so they were definitely feeling that over and over," she said.

The exploring of new textures seemed to please Kramer more than the other raccoons, and the paintings that volunteers liked were put aside. Before long, there were several dozen paintings, and even Payne, who had started it all more or less as a joke, had to admit they were attractive.

"The very first painting still hangs in the nursery at the rehab. It actually looked like something. Her first masterpiece was a yellow, red, blue, and green abstract piece called *The Rooster*," Payne said.

No one is certain whose idea it was to offer the paintings by Kramer and peers for sale to the public. Everyone admits the first "Raccoon art sale" was done with tongue firmly planted in cheek at the Hope for Wildlife Open House in late August. Some workers thought the joke was being taken a bit too far.

"Then we saw the reaction of the people at the open house. They sold all of them, every one we had, at that first open house. They were just flying off the table. I mean, I really wanted to get one, but I didn't get a chance to sneak in until later and they'd all been sold," Bond said.

From there, word of this new art form started to spread. Someone would see a genuine Kramer in a home or office and decide they had to have one. Custom orders with specifications for colours started to come in. Payne took over production and orders as a regular part of her work, and the paintings went on sale permanently in the rehab centre gift shop. Suddenly, Kramer was to raccoon art as Monet had been to French Impressionism.

In theory, once a school of art has been established, you don't need the master anymore, and that was true with Kramer. Raccoon art was well established in September when her eyesight unexpectedly cleared up. Like many coddled or spoiled animals, she was used to getting her own way, and what Kramer now wanted was freedom. She got to be cranky and hard to handle—a regular maturing raccoon—so when her peers were sent to the wild in late September, she went with them. Bond and the other summer workers were gone by then, but were happy for Kramer when they heard.

"Truthfully, it's best for them to be out in the wild. They are wild animals. I knew she would have been very comfortable if she'd stayed at the rehab because everyone would have spoiled her, but it was so much more exciting to hear she had got her sight back and gone back to the wild," said Bond.

Kramer's departure did not stop the flow of raccoon art. She became a legendary centrepiece, the blind, orphan artist who started it, and every year since, a few new raccoons showed talent and continued her work. The demand did not ebb either. Hope Swinimer kept a few paintings next to her office desk at the Dartmouth Veterinary Hospital, just in case. Payne set up a display in a convenience store where she had winter work and sold everything she had, making over $700 for the centre.

The successful sales and their contribution to the always tight Hope for Wildlife finances were appreciated by Swinimer, but did not prepare her for the shocker that came in 2009. She and the rest of her staff were taken aback early that year when Adrianna Afford of Argyle Fine Art in Halifax's Historic Properties contacted them. Would Hope for Wildlife like to stage a raccoon art exhibition over the upcoming March break?

The idea had come from a client of the gallery who knew Swinimer and her work. She was aware of what was going on with the raccoon art and explained it to Afford.

There are good reasons why it is illegal to keep a raccoon as a pet. This is the cute kit stage. In less than six months, raccoons become dangerous and very difficult to handle.

"She sort of pitched the idea to me. It was so strange and interesting, so I just thought, what the heck, we'll just try it," said Afford.

Afford chose March break to open the show in the hopes that more families would come, and visitors poured in as the week progressed, helped substantially by newspaper, television, and radio coverage of the story of Hope for Wildlife, Kramer, and raccoon art. Everything built towards the Saturday, when Swinimer announced she would be there with her saw-whet owl, Seesaw. Argyle Fine Art had never seen a crowd that size for an event.

"It was packed. The whole day was packed," Afford reported. "It was the middle of March, not the nicest time of the year, and a cold day, but we had families and children and piles of people showing up everywhere."

According to Afford, it was more than just a chance to buy raccoon art; it brought in people curious to find out what Hope for Wildlife was all about.

"Hearing the story behind how this all began, that was really intriguing for people. It kind of started some really interesting conversations that probably wouldn't come up normally in our gallery," Afford said.

Swinimer was unprepared for the diversity of the people who came out for the show. Paintings were sold, others custom ordered,

A THIEF, AND A SMART ONE

Because their nimble forepaws resemble hands and black facial markings look like a mask, raccoons have been mythologized as very capable thieves. That reputation, it turns out, may be more truth than legend. Recent studies have shown that a raccoon can remember for up to three years a series of tasks needed to get into a food source.

but like Afford, the Hope for Wildlife founder believed it was the conversation that stood out.

"I think people came to the show not only to see what we had to offer, but to tell us their raccoon stories," she said. "That was a lot of fun because everybody has a raccoon story or two to share."

For Nicole Payne, whose idea started raccoon art as a means of entertaining a young, blind raccoon named Kramer, there is no end in sight for this story. Every year she offers fingerpaint to all the new kits, looking for the ones who will be that year's artists. When they are found, they can no longer simply splash around with random colours. Custom orders with very specific demands have taken over. In 2009, a woman in Nova Scotia sent each of her grand-children in British Columbia paintings in their favourite colours.

"People are asking for custom orders to match specific rooms in their homes," Payne explained. "I'm in the process of getting together two paintings for a woman in Ontario who wants one as large as possible that matches the colours in her den and another that matches her nursery colours to hang in her unborn daughter's room."

Custom-ordered art? Perhaps it is just a matter of time before a scholar or journalist treks though the woods of Nova Scotia, hoping to find Kramer to get her opinion on what the new generation has done to her art form.

On the other hand, perhaps Hope Swinimer comes closer to the truth:

"I think it's been a brilliant idea," she said. "People find it fun. To me, it's been a way to bring humour into what we do every day, a way to lighten the negatives of our world."

CHAPTER 6

A DIFFERENT KIND OF CAT

The most abundant wild member of the cat family in Nova Scotia is the bobcat. In fact, the province is recognized as the best bobcat habitat in Canada, with about one for every twelve square kilometres. Usually, a bobcat is twice the size of a domestic cat, with a weight between eleven and fourteen kilograms, but on the edges of towns and cities, where feral domestic cats and bobcats overlap their range, it is not uncommon at night, dusk, or dawn for large domestics and small bobcats to be mistaken for each other.

CLIFFORD

The couple's first reaction was surprise, then pity. They were out for an evening drive on a dirt road through the woods behind Lake Echo when they saw one more example of humankind's inhumanity toward animals. A single lost kitten, at best three weeks old, sat beside the road looking very frightened. Knowing the animal could not survive here where a callous owner had obviously dumped him, they scooped up the terrified tyke, by this point wild with fear, and took him home with them to raise as a pet.

They soon realized their mistake. Quick razor-sharp claws and knife-like teeth, coupled with a disposition wilder than a housecat on its worst day, told them that what they had brought into their home was a young bobcat. They called Hope for Wildlife.

"He was feisty," remembered Hope Swinimer. "Even though he was just tiny and still had his blue eyes, he knew enough to be scared of people. He was just terrified. They soon figured it out and gave me a call, so we went and collected the little spitfire."

For Swinimer, there were several important questions she would have liked answers to but knew she would never get. Why was the kitten beside the road? Had the couple interrupted the mother cat moving him? Was the mother dead? If so, what had happened to her and how long had her baby been on its own? Swinimer had what she thought was a best guess on the matter.

"We just don't know. Maybe this was a case where people should not have interfered. But the cat was not using his hind end very well, and that is usually a sign of rickets and poor diet. If it had been with its mom right up to that point, I don't think it would have had that problem. Something tells me that little one must have been separated from its mom for longer than a day. The mother could have been hit by a car and gone off to die in the woods."

For a bobcat, this was a late baby. He was found the first week in August, and his kind usually gives birth anywhere from February to late May. Bobcats are single parent families and their litters are small, with only one or two kittens. This helps the mother, who raises them on her own. Their versatile diet is also an asset to her. A bobcat will kill and eat anything from a large insect to a small deer, although its food of choice in Nova Scotia is the snowshoe hare.

The workers at Hope for Wildlife were surprised at how small the cat was for so late in the year. It was obvious there had been a diet problem, but he showed no interest in any of the food offered him at Swinimer's shelter, leaving her with only one option. It would require two brave people.

"We had to force feed him at first. We needed a good, nutritious food to help with the rickets, so we were syringe feeding him, forcing it down his throat," she said.

The job fell to Swinimer and her friend Reid. They had in the past dealt with several aggressive animals, but this one, despite his tiny size, proved a handful.

Clifford and Gretel.

"We had to wear heavy, heavy gloves, or else we would get bitten quite badly, even though he was just a little thing," Swinimer admitted.

Hope for Wildlife had fostered predators before and knew that they required special treatment, even one this size. One important thing was to isolate the young bobcat, now called Clifford, from the types of birds and animals that would one day become his prey. His age and health were also potential problems, so Swinimer moved him to her house, away from the rehabilitation centre and regular pens. It wasn't the first time she had done this with an animal, and she set up a very quiet room where no one went in and out. Her house also had connecting outside pens, if needed. They were for special cases, and this was a special case. On several levels, for several reasons, imprinting is a concern when dealing with a young predator such as a bobcat.

"There are two kinds of imprinting. There is imprinting where they come to think humans are their family, and they don't know they are a cat. Then there is the type of imprinting where they just bond with one person and hate everybody else. That's not so dangerous. That's not such a bad thing. I was hoping if Reid and I were the only ones caring for Clifford, he'd be fearful of everyone

IN THE BEGINNING

The bobcat's ancestor, an ancient predecessor of the Eurasian lynx, first came to North America across the Bering Land Bridge about 2.5 million years ago. Glaciers eventually confined that cat population to the southern half of North America, where it evolved into the modern bobcat. Meanwhile, another migration of lynx crossed from Asia but was confined to what is now Alaska by the same glaciations. This migration evolved into the Canadian lynx.

else to a certain degree. Maybe there wasn't too much logic to that, but I thought it was for the best," explained Swinimer.

In his first weeks at the rehabilitation centre, the little bobcat was not called Clifford. In fact, according to a vote taken by visitors to the Hope for Wildlife open house that August, he still isn't, wherever he is. Clifford was Swinimer's name choice but her companion, Reid, preferred Cecil. For a while, both were used, neither side would give in, and it was put to what was supposed to be a binding vote by open-house guests. Cecil won by a landslide, so the cat became Clifford.

"Owning the facility has some privileges," Swinimer explained.

Clifford grew up in Swinimer's house, totally isolated from the Hope for Wildlife world that surrounded it. There was, however, another animal that resided there, the pine marten Gretel and as a mature, female predator, albeit from a distinctly smaller species, Gretel took it upon herself to teach the bobcat kitten his place.

"At first the pine marten was bigger than the bobcat," Swinimer remembered, "so Gretel would boss him and chase him, and I let them interact because it was stimulation, and also it taught him play, which I'm sure his mother would have done. At first it was fun to watch. Gretel would be really mean to Clifford, grab his ears and really yank him around the room."

Then one day everything changed, and the two never played together again. Swinimer didn't see what happened, but she had a good idea why the behaviour shifted.

"I think Clifford just said 'Okay, I'm bigger than you now, I'm the boss!' and he let her know that. From that day forward, Gretel was scared to even go near Clifford."

As Clifford slowly matured, it was easy to see that while his species and domestic cats had been sundered for millions of years, there were still some similarities. Bobcats respond to affection like cats do. They purr, groom, and like having their ears scratched, Swinimer observed. They also have similar temperaments. From her work as manager of the Dartmouth Veterinary Hospital, Swinimer knew very well that cats are "independent, they don't want to be bossed by anyone." Clifford was no different. Hope for Wildlife handled him cautiously because they knew as he grew more mature, he would react aggressively if forced to do something he didn't want to. Any attempt to discipline or punish him would have resulted in a very violent confrontation, so that was avoided.

This became more and more of an issue because bobcats stay with their mothers for a full year. They overwinter as part of a family group, learning to be adults by hunting, which meant Clifford would be much more mature than most Hope for Wildlife fosterlings when his release time came. Swinimer and her crew were going to have to deal with an adolescent male bobcat. Eventually, he grew to the point where he was moved regularly from the house to a large outside unit, and as time went by, that became a problem.

"He was strong and dominant from the start," according to Swinimer, "and that was good, because it would help him survive in the wild. But he could do serious harm, and just because he knew us, didn't mean he would spare us. He could rip us to pieces if we didn't know what we were doing. Eighty per cent of the time he was fine, because we weren't trying to force him to do anything. It was just when you tried to get him into a unit, or move him when he didn't want to be moved."

But Clifford had to be moved. If he was going to be released the following spring, learning to hunt became a priority, as did getting used to outdoor weather. Then there was the matter of visitors to Swinimer's home. Clifford, as a permanent house guest who had known discipline only from a pine marten, and then only until he outgrew it, was very demanding on humans who dropped in. If they came into his domain, they could either pet him or serve his

A maturing Clifford, aloof in the barn rafters.

other need: they could be his scratching post. Deirdre Dwyer was working with Hope for Wildlife that summer, helping set up their new education centre. She remembers her frequent visits to the house for conversations with Swinimer.

"I used to wear shorts, and I'd come back from the house with my legs covered in scratches," she said. "If Clifford wanted something, he let you know. I mentioned to Hope that she would soon have to look at getting him out of there, and she agreed."

Learning to hunt was another major priority. As a cat from the wild, Clifford obviously had the instincts to kill his food. Even domestic cats, his far distant cousins, still have those, and will readily exercise them on birds and backyard rodents when the chance arises.

However, Clifford not only needed to learn that he had those instincts, he required practice hunting so that he could support himself when he was set free. A dead rat served by a Hope for Wildlife volunteer was supper, but take away that human and a young bobcat had to realize that food came alive, not thawed. He needed to hone his hunting and killing skills so he could provide for himself. Clifford could become a killer—that was undeniable—but required something to practice on.

"We very seldom use live prey, but there are cases where we have to. Young birds of prey must learn to hunt, so you just have to do this kind of thing," explained Swinimer. "The same with bobcats. Most of the time, we're off the hook on this. You don't have to teach a squirrel how to eat. You don't have to teach a white-tailed deer. But there are certain species you do, so you have to go through that process."

Swinimer did not ask many volunteers to take part in live feedings. She and Reid handled it themselves. For the most part, Clifford's food was rats and mice, but bobcats have a very diverse diet, and Clifford needed to recognize the edible creatures he might meet in the wild. Injured birds brought to the shelter that were obviously suffering and could not be saved were readily available.

"Death is quick with a bobcat," Swinimer said. "If it meant choosing between sticking a bird with a needle or a quick death in a bobcat unit, at least it would serve a natural purpose."

A typical adolescent, Clifford showed no willingness to cooperate in his education, and this sometimes proved not only exasperating but also humourous. On one occasion, a local farmer let it be known that some of his hens had stopped laying and he was going to wring their necks. Would Hope for Wildlife like dead chickens for the animals? Swinimer and her team immediately thought of Clifford. He had not yet killed for food, but if locked in a cage with a live chicken, could finish it much more humanely than a neck-wringing would, plus it would break the food kill barrier. On a winter's evening, Swinimer slipped one of the farmer's chickens into the bobcat cage and locked the door. She had given Clifford his big chance. The next morning she returned to find a very alive hen casually walking up and down one side of the cage, pecking, with an indifferent Clifford on the other side. The chicken was retrieved, nicknamed "Lucky" on the spot, and became an untouchable guest for the rest of her days, popular with children visiting the rehab centre.

Clifford did learn to hunt that first winter, but in typical cat fashion, he did it his way. Swinimer was watching him in his pen one day when a red squirrel arrived outside, noted Clifford's food, and darted inside for a treat. It was his last attempted theft. Clifford was on him in a flash, so quickly and efficiently that Swinimer felt sure it could not have been his first kill. In any case, she was satisfied that her bobcat boy had grown into a predator and found it somewhat pleasing that after months of her trying to find a thing for him to kill, he had done it on his own.

The arrival of Clifford as a mature predator corresponded with spring and the season of new babies, and while he had been one of those handfuls himself the previous year, he now stood apart. That year's orphans were potential food for a second year bobcat, and they seemed to sense the danger in him. For the new volunteers arriving at Hope for Wildlife, the experience was similar. It was the season of newborn cuteness, and sweet little fox kits, fawns, and raccoon cubs were what they expected. Laura Bond was one of the new workers learning how to clean cages.

"I'll always remember the awe I felt on my first day of work coming face to face with a full grown bobcat," she said. "When Allison told me she was taking me into the cage of a bobcat kitten, I thought Clifford would be about the size of a house cat, not the size of a large dog. When he came out to investigate who was coming onto his territory, I remember thinking, 'You have got to be kidding me. I'm supposed to clean the cage with *this* in it?' It is very unusual for me to get nervous around any animal. I usually have no fear. But at that point I wanted to yell at Allison, to ask her if she realized she was standing two feet away from a full grown bobcat!"

Summer came, Clifford was a full year old, and according to the way of bobcats everywhere, it was time for him to go off to make his own life. Of course, there were fears at Hope for Wildlife. They had done their best, but he had not been raised by another bobcat and all his humans could do was hope that what they were capable of would be enough. To cushion the blow, Swinimer and company decided on a soft release.

With a hard release, an animal is taken far from people into a wilderness area and set free to cope on its own. This was commonly done with deer. However, in a soft release, the animal is let go into familiar surroundings, in Clifford's case the Seaforth facility where he had been raised. The gate to his pen remained open so he could return if he ran into a problem, and food was provided in case his initial hunting didn't go well. Since Clifford had spent so many of his first weeks in the farmhouse, a pantry window was raised every night, just in case.

It would be a mistake to say that Clifford had become a pet and that was why a soft release was chosen. He had required personal attention as a predator, and over two years that had likely involved

A bobcat at play shows that, despite millions of years apart, it is still in many ways close to its domestic cousin.

some degree of imprinting, but that had been minimized, and it was never Swinimer's intention to keep him permanently. There were, and still are, places in North America where that can be done with bobcats, but they don't make good pets. A bobcat is a nocturnal predator and as a house pet it will roam all night and hunt anything that moves. The end result is not good for other pets. A mature bobcat marks its territory with urine, not popular with most people. Strangers in a house with a resident bobcat must be very careful because these cats are extremely territorial, and twice as large as a feline. Then there's the matter of health. If your pet injures someone, you can always take them to a hospital. For domestic pets, you take them to a vet, but most veterinarians won't treat bobcats.

Behind the Seaforth farm are miles of wilderness, a landscape filled with forests, marshes, lakes, hills, and rivers—perfect bobcat habitat. Sooner or later, as his confidence grew, everyone believed Clifford would feel the pull of the wilderness.

"It was funny how it worked out," said Swinimer. "He hung around for a good month or more. Almost every day, we would see him. Sometimes he would come up to us, but oftentimes he would be evasive and not approach. But many, many nights he'd come in around two o'clock through the pantry window, up to our bedroom,

THE LYNX FAMILY

There are today four species in the lynx family of cats, including the Eurasian lynx, Spanish lynx, Canadian lynx, and bobcat. The Eurasian lynx is by far the largest, averaging twenty-five kilograms, with its Siberian subspecies sometimes reaching forty kilograms. The bobcat is the smallest at about thirteen kilograms.

jump on the bed, give us a purr and a lick, sleep for a while, and then be gone in the morning before we woke up. We'd always know he'd been there, because he'd wake us up."

By late summer, Clifford was a young bobcat in his prime. Swinimer would still see him early every morning when she fed the deer in their pen, and more than for any other human, he still showed her respect, friendship, and trust. There came a day, however, when even that changed. One morning when she went to the deer pens, there was Clifford, just outside the wire, stalking the deer. He was in full predator mode, and the herd's natural fear of a carnivore had kicked in.

"He was really upsetting them, stressing them, and you really don't want to stress your white-tailed deer," Swinimer said. "It was an eight-foot-high wire fence. I didn't think he'd climb it, but I suppose he could have, and I was kind of worried. And I was late for work."

Swinimer reacted as she did when any of her animals threatened to cause a disaster. She isolated him from the problem.

"I didn't want to sit at work for twelve hours worrying about whether Clifford was in the deer pen, and I knew I would if I just left this situation the way it was playing out here. So I just grabbed him, threw him into his old holding unit, and left him there all day."

She received neither a bite nor a scratch. The bobcat still trusted her, but it would be the last time. Clifford's old holding pen was the one adjacent to the house and the pantry window. Swinimer rushed off to her job at the Dartmouth Veterinary Hospital thinking the situ-

Clifford may have had what appeared to be housecat moments, but the wild was always in him and eventually took over.

ation was under control and that she could straighten it out when she got home. However, she had forgotten to close the window. When she returned that evening, Swinimer could see Clifford inside the house, and what she saw was not the bobcat she knew. He was pacing back and forth with the mechanical, frustrated gait of a caged predator and when she opened the door, Clifford blew by her and was gone.

"I never saw Clifford again," said Swinimer. "I don't know if it was locking him up and taking away his freedom for that twelve-hour period, but he never, ever came back. We still left our pantry window open for a good year and a half, but he never returned."

As far as completing the task started with a tiny kitten more than a year before, the work had been done. Clifford was an adult and in the forest, avoiding humans of his own volition. He was, as far as anyone knew, wild and well.

The humans who knew him, however, kept open windows in their hearts long after he was gone. Allison Dube said people wanted to think of Clifford as alive and happy.

"Every time we pick up a dead or injured bobcat, we shudder and sort of freak out," Dube said. "We never tagged him, so in the end we'll never know, but with Clifford, I guess I don't really want to know."

CHAPTER 7

BECAUSE WE CAN

The job that hawks, eagles, and other diurnal raptors do during the day, owls take care of at night. Most of their diet is small rodents. While the day hunters use speed and eyesight to get their prey, owls rely on silence and acute hearing. Their wings have special feathers on the leading edge that slow their flight but baffle any noise, making them so silent that legends have long linked them to the supernatural. Their hearing is such that a great grey can slip from a perch and crash through a thick snow crust to take an unseen mouse in a tunnel. Most common in Nova Scotia is the barred owl. These owls stalk the fringes of our highways, especially in winter when scurrying food all too often distracts them from speeding vehicles.

SALTY

The driver never saw what the owl was chasing. The bird itself had been nothing more than a glimpse of grey in the fraction of a second when its course intersected with that of the salt truck. It was there and then it was not. Somewhere in between was a sickening thump, followed by the tableau of a man kneeling beside a broken barred owl in the winter darkness on a Shelburne County road.

MANY NAMES

Because its range now extends across North America and as far south as central Mexico, the barred owl has many local names. These include hoot owl, eight hooter, rain owl, wood owl, swamp owl, striped owl, round-headed owl, and in French, *le chat-huant du nord*.

Truck–barred owl collisions usually mean a broken wing, but not this time. The owl had no time to brace for the shock and rammed into the vehicle head first, leaving its face a mangled wreck. The upper beak was crushed, bloody, and pointing sideways, while the lower one was intact but the jaw behind it horribly smashed, causing it to be counter to the top part's direction. The salt truck driver stared at the crumpled bird, devastated, then placed its unconscious form alongside him on the vehicle's front seat and drove home. Once there, he began to look for help.

The next day was November 22, 2008, and things were not going well at Hope for Wildlife. Hope Swinimer and her companion, Reid Patterson, had done something bold in open defiance of the eccentric spirits who govern wildlife rehabilitation and in all foolishness actually expected to get away with it. They had scheduled a trip to the Amazon rain forest, their first vacation in many years, and of course, since this was the day they were scheduled to leave, malicious forces were busily at work. In Bedford, someone lit and closed their wood stove, only to whip it open again to remove a flaming flying squirrel. A great horned owl was reported badly injured, and staffer Nicole Payne immediately rushed to the rescue before Swinimer could begin to contemplate cancelling her trip. Now there came the call from Shelburne about a barred owl whose face was destroyed in a one-sided duel with a salt truck. While these were being dealt with, two more calls came in. It took a major effort to convince Swinimer the situation was under control and that she could, with a clear conscience, get on the plane.

Many of the animals Hope for Wildlife gathered that day had very serious injuries, so while Swinimer sped south for her vacation, her workers were arriving at the Dartmouth Veterinary Hospital looking for Dr. Barry MacEachern. Payne was there, holding her rescued great horned while it was euthanized. Its wing had been shattered in several places and was not repairable. While there, she met the South Shore owl that became known as Salty, and which would dominate her time for most of the next year.

Despite injuries so severe and repair work so delicate that recovery seemed to verge on the impossible, Dr. MacEachern decided to attempt making Salty capable of not only living but also being wild again. When she returned from her Amazon adventure, Swinimer immediately understood how unusual and intricate the task MacEachern had undertaken was going to be.

"Looking at that bird, I'll bet ninety-nine point nine per cent of veterinarians would have euthanized on the spot. His whole beak was smashed and he was in pretty bad shape," she commented.

Payne had been directly involved from the beginning and saw MacEachern's decision as an important milestone for the young doctor, who had enough confidence in his skills to go beyond expectations and take risks.

"If it had been a year earlier, Salty probably would have been just euthanized immediately," she explained. "The difference was Barry getting more familiar with raptor physiology and veterinary care. He just decided to go for it and give it a try, and he got it right."

The fact that Salty was a barred owl made the situation more sensitive. Most raptors live by their talons. These powerful feet enable them to hunt and kill successfully. Their beaks are secondary tools, used mainly for ripping larger prey into chunks that can be swallowed. A barred owl is different. Its power is almost evenly distributed between beak and talons, creating a hunting package in which the feet are slightly weaker than those of many other raptors but the beak much stronger. There are claims that a barred owl's beak can crack a turtle's shell, making it far more than simply a dining instrument. Carried along by silent wings with a span of up to 126 centimetres, the result is a very effective night hunter. It was obvious to anyone who knew owls that to succeed, MacEachern's repairs on Salty could be nothing less than perfect.

The decision by the veterinarian to attempt the surgery was not made without careful consideration of the larger picture of Salty's health. MacEachern knew it would be a long-term project, but the crucial period was quite short, and after that it was just going to be a matter of continual tinkering and adjustment.

"With that particular case, because nothing else was wrong with the owl, I felt it was worth giving it a try. We'd know within a few weeks to a month if it was going to work. Once we knew the bill was growing out, it was just going to be a toying thing," MacEachern said.

The lower jaw, or mandible, was the first problem. It was broken in two places on the same side. This required very careful setting if the beak was to work smoothly and accurately again. If the upper beak regrew, its lower partner had to be in precise position to meet it, and the mandible would have to be set immediately for it to do so, even though it would be months before the top section's final position was known. The broken mandible was set together with a pin, but that was only the beginning. In order to heal properly, it had to be kept from moving, so surgical wiring was used to support the pinning, and that in turn had to be stabilized.

"There were wires there almost like braces, and just so it wasn't disturbed, we taped the mouth shut so that it could only open about half a centimetre," explained MacEachern.

The problem with the upper bill was completely different, for the damage was not to the bone but to the bill itself. A raptor's bill is made of keratin, the same substance as human fingernails and toenails, and although much thicker, is subject to the same type of injuries. In Salty's case, the bill had been destroyed. The first half-inch was completely gone, and the rest was heavily damaged right up and into the growing point under the feathers. This included a split that went almost to the root of the bill, and as with a human nail, the only thing to do was to cut away the damaged material and hope it grew back.

"I trimmed most of that off because a lot of it was dying," MacEachern said. The crack was the major concern, according to the doctor, "but I didn't think it went all the way to the growing portion of the bill, so that's why we gave it a chance."

To be certain only undamaged material survived, the upper bill was sanded back to almost nothing.

Raptor specialist Nicole Payne handles an injured barred owl. Note how the heavy towel prevents the wings from moving, while her hands inside the towel wrap control the talons.

"We used a Dremel drill, and as it grew, we just filed it into a normal bill shape. If we hadn't, because the lower bill was fully grown and the normal shape, the upper probably would have hit it at some point and grown into an abnormal position since all the points weren't coming together at the same time," explained MacEachern.

At three weeks, x-rays showed the lower jaw was healing, and at six, the tape, wires, and pins were removed. Salty's mandible was declared healed and now the long wait began while a new upper beak slowly grew and was shaped. The work done by Dr. MacEachern so far appeared perfect, and it was now just a matter

Because it is very shortsighted, an owl needs specialized touch-sensitive feathers in order to eat.

of watching to see if the two halves would come together and function. The owl was taken to Hope for Wildlife on New Year's Day to start rehabilitation work, and the staff there celebrated his arrival, especially Nicole Payne. Actually, Payne's celebration was more about going than arriving. All through the surgery and healing of his jaw, Salty had been camping in the laundry room of her father's Cole Harbour home, right next door to her bedroom. It was her job to feed an owl whose jaw was pinned, wired, and taped shut, at the same time making certain nothing touched or otherwise disturbed Dr. MacEachern's handiwork. With Swinimer away, Payne knew of no other way to keep the bird safe except to have him as a house guest.

"I was one of only two people on staff at the time familiar with even handling a raptor, let alone feeding it," Payne said. "It was about six weeks of constant nursing three times per day at my home. He stayed in the room next to mine, and I would get up in the middle of the night and go feed him."

FEATHERS THAT FEEL

Owls may have tremendous night vision, but once they catch their prey, they can't see it. They are extremely nearsighted. However, they have an unusual ability that allows them to handle food. Their talons and beaks have very sensitive hair-like feathers called filoplumes that act as feelers. Instead of seeing what they eat, they feel it.

Salty's menu consisted of only one thing: a recovery cat food formula given to felines coming off major surgery. It stank like rotten fish in its solid state, but Payne had to mix it with warm water, mash it to a liquid, suck it into a large syringe, insert a metal tube down the bird's throat, and inject the lot into his stomach three times each day without aspirating him. The stench sickened her, but Salty loved the stuff and soon started demanding it.

Feeding the owl was difficult at first, especially in the middle of the night when he was naturally awake and Payne asleep. Because he was fully alert then, Payne included his medications during this feeding, grinding up pills to a fine powder and serving them mixed into the vile food he was so fond of. Getting the feeding tube around the surgery and down his throat posed the biggest problem.

"At first it was difficult," Payne said. "I'd have to hold his head without hurting the jaw, which was hard because part of the wiring went right up to the corner where the mandible joins the skull. When we have a raptor for feeding, we often hold them in those joints and force their mouth open, but I couldn't do that, so I'd try to hold the back of his head, without touching that joint. Then I'd gently tip his head back so he'd try to open his mouth to protest, and I'd slide the tube down, trying to feed him in a swift, fluid motion, without also having it go down into his lungs."

Once the hardware was off, Payne was responsible for getting the owl back on solid food so he could be penned at Hope for

A barred owl's dark brown eyes give it a less aggressive appearance. It is the only owl in this part of the world with brown eyes.

Wildlife's Seaforth facility. She started him with meat pieces he could swallow whole without ripping or tearing with the damaged bill. Payne thought she was giving him a treat when she bought pre-cut stir-fry meats for him.

"He did not want anything to do with it. He wanted his cat food. It was like trying to force a three year old to eat his vegetables," she remembered. "He'd clamp up his beak and just keep turning it up and away, as if he was saying 'No, no, I don't want it. I'm not going to eat that.' By the end of feeding him that vile cat food, it was as easy as opening up the box and he'd be ready, waiting for it. But once the meat came, it was like starting over again."

FEAR AND WORSHIP

From the beginning of human history, owls were feared and worshipped, and words connected to them found their way into English in many strange ways. For example, the Icelandic word for owl is *ugla*, which gave another word to that language, *uggligr*. This became the Scandinavian *ugly*, which came to English in the Middle Ages. Actually, the Icelandic *uggligr* shows perfectly the ancient connection to owl mythology and worship. It means "something to be feared."

Salty continued to hold out for cat food even when he was moved back to Seaforth. Because it was the middle of the winter and he had spent a month and a half indoors, he was penned with a heat lamp along with his food and water, but he still refused to eat. Even mice could not tempt him. It was Reid Patterson who made the breakthrough. He had caught smelts and put some live ones in Salty's pen, which ended the food strike immediately. As soon as a smelt started flopping, he was on them and the cat food was forgotten.

It was September before the bill crisis worked itself out. Dr. MacEachern kept the top section filed flat as it grew so it would not deform itself against the lower bill. Once it passed the tip of the mature segment, its natural hook was allowed to develop and, to everyone's delight, the sections came together perfectly. MacEachern's work had created a new and functioning tool for Salty, one that would let him have his life in the wild back again.

It was on a September evening when Payne and a few others dropped in to visit Dr. MacEachern where he was camped at Porter's Lake Provincial Park. Payne had a cardboard box with her and in it was Salty.

Salty up close, his damaged beak starting to heal.

"We found Barry's campsite and it was good and dark by that time," said Payne. "Everyone gathered around. I took Salty out of his box, tucked him under my arm, and he behaved nicely, allowing Barry and I to pet and say goodbye to him. Then I just gave him a little toss and he flew right up into a tree. He stayed there for a little bit, scoped things out, then off he went into the night."

There were many at Hope for Wildlife and in the veterinary profession who were impressed with how Salty's story ended. Dr. MacEachern's remarkable surgery and Nicole Payne's dedicated care had saved a bird so badly injured that in any other time or place he would likely have been immediately euthanized.

It should always be remembered that Salty was not a pet but a wild, ownerless bird. There was no one to pay for the services he received. Certainly there was no guarantee that once set loose, he would have any more luck surviving than other creatures living by the laws of the forest. Salty may have flown only a few hundred metres that night and been killed by a great horned owl. Or he may have headed for the nearest highway and flown into another truck. None of that matters.

What does matter is that two people saw a wild creature with its life in jeopardy, thought they could help it, and were willing to try.

CHAPTER 8

WE APPEAR TO HAVE A PROBLEM

> "Patience is the best remedy for every trouble."
> Titus Maccius Plautus (c. 254–184 BC)

Ask anyone at Hope for Wildlife's Seaforth rehabilitation centre: the Roman playwright would never have written that if he had met Lucifer. Patience has had no effect whatsoever on getting this troublesome raccoon free and far away. There seems to be no explanation for his problem, other than calling it, and him, an anomaly.

LUCIFER

The summer of 2009 was a rough one at Hope for Wildlife. An outbreak of panleukopenia, a rapid and deadly viral disease also known as feline distemper, was running amok in the raccoon pens, decimating that spring's masked orphans and pressing their small on-site animal hospital into double service as both a triage centre and isolation ward. When a phone call came from Truro about more raccoon orphans, Swinimer was already caught between a dozen disasters and a handful of catastrophes, and later acknowledged she likely didn't give it her full attention. What she missed was the announcement that a soon-to-be legendary troublemaker was about to arrive.

"The gentleman said he had two orphaned baby raccoons, and both were without hair," Swinimer remembered. "I didn't think too much about it. It was really busy that day, and I get so many strange phone calls. I told him to bring them in, but I was just run off my feet and was really, really tired, and Nicole [Payne] happened to be here. I asked her to look after him when he arrived."

The man was there quickly with his two sons and a pet carrier. They had found the animals in their backyard and left for Seaforth as soon as he got off the phone with Swinimer. No one considered their haste in any way unusual, perhaps because everyone was too busy to really think about it, so Payne took them on a tour of the Hope for Wildlife facility and then they were gone. The carrier was taken to the hospital to have its contents assessed, vaccinated, and fed. Payne was an experienced wildlife rehab worker, but was in for a shock. When she opened the pet carrier, inside were two young raccoons with perfectly normal fur on their heads and tails, even down to the trademark mask and stripes. The rest of each body, however, was naked.

"They were quite large and well developed, probably close to two months old," she said, "totally normal raccoons for that age, except for the fact that they were almost completely hairless. They had by far the least amount of fur I had ever seen on a raccoon."

Not only were they hairless, they were also very bad-tempered, especially the one she later named Lucifer. Payne knew trouble when she saw it, and realized the arrivals would only add to the crushing weight of existing raccoon problems. She started an emergency search for her boss, carrying with her the news that in the midst of an epidemic that was killing dozens of their raccoons every week, two new ones with hairless bodies had just been deposited on them.

Swinimer later admitted she didn't grasp what she was told. When Payne announced they now had two bald raccoons, she assumed it was just figurative language, forgetting what the man who had dropped them off had said on the phone. Even when the puzzled messenger repeated it twice, there was no reaction.

"I've seen raccoons before with very little hair. You know, when they are orphaned, they have a hard time of it, and they can show it," Swinimer explained.

The lack of response from her leader surprised Payne. These were not normal raccoons, and she knew it, but the question now was whether Swinimer had known it when she agreed to take the pair.

UP TO SCRATCH

The name "raccoon" is thought to come from the Algonquin First Nation. It is an English mispronunciation of their word *arukun*, meaning "he who scratches with his hands."

In a matter-of-fact manner, Swinimer made her way to the medical centre to view the newcomers, but she wasn't there long. A few minutes later she was running back to Payne.

"Nicole, those raccoons are bald!" Swinimer blurted out.

Payne was speechless for a moment, and then replied, "Uh, isn't that what I told you? Three times?"

There was another pause, broken by Swinimer, whom Payne could see was still in disbelief.

"But Nicole, those raccoons have no hair!" she said.

"I know, Hope. That's why I told you they were bald," responded Payne.

Swinimer at last understood the difference between what she expected and what had actually arrived.

"I thought you meant they had a bald spot or something!" she sighed.

More than 150 raccoons died of panleukopenia that summer at Hope for Wildlife, and newcomers like Lucifer and his brother were kept isolated and away from the tragedy underway in the main pens. They did not have the virus when they arrived and never got it. However, while Lucifer thrived, put on weight, got into trouble every moment he could, and remained a nasty character, his brother turned out to have other serious health problems and died in a matter of weeks. Since local veterinarians were as puzzled as the rehab workers about the baldness, the dead raccoon was sent away for a professional necropsy. While they waited for the test results, the daily parade past Lucifer's cage continued. Everyone agreed there wasn't a new hair showing anywhere.

When the report came back, it was a huge disappointment. No reason was found for the raccoon's failure to grow fur, leading a

Raccoon kits feeding. For some reason, racoons have proved the most difficult species to wean.

sarcastic Payne to summarize it as "Congratulations, you've got a bald raccoon!" They had hoped for an answer that would help them understand Lucifer, but this did nothing for them, as Hope for Wildlife had no previous experience with bald mammals. There had been a bald crow named Rudy who finally grew feathers after nine months, so he became the standard Lucifer was judged by.

"I guess my brain was thinking that it happened with Rudy, so it would happen to Lucifer, but so far there is nothing, not even a little bit. We used to stand there, stare at him, and ask each other if we thought he was growing fur. But he wasn't growing anything. He's still not," said Swinimer later as Lucifer entered his second year as her guest. "Until you actually see him, you can't comprehend how ridiculous he looks. He's ugly, a pretty sad looking character."

Very young raccoons need to be tube fed, but getting food into Lucifer was not easy. Staff member Hayley Inkpen said his personality and lack of hair both contributed.

"He was a terror to feed. He was squirmy and would give the worst bites, and it was hard because he had no fur, so there was nothing to really hold him by," Inkpen said. "The amount of times he got away from me, jumped to the floor, and ran would be too many to count."

Partially or totally bald raccoons were rare, but had been recorded before, and was usually attributed to mange, a common condition that causes fur loss in animals. However, this was not the case with Lucifer, nor with some of the totally hairless raccoons found occasionally in the southern United States, where the climate gave them a better chance for survival.

Biologists studied those southern cases carefully and classified raccoons lacking fur but not having mange as "anomalies," things that didn't fit normal classification. Their work was made urgent by a new and rapidly spreading Latin American myth. Since the 1990s, there had been a wave of stories, at first oral but then picked up by news media, about "el chupacabara," a hairless night monster that sucked blood from farm animals. The myth was first heard in Puerto Rico in 1995, and in fifteen years had spread as far south as Chile and north to Maine. Even though several so-called chupacabara sightings in Texas turned out to be either mangy foxes or hairless raccoon anomalies, the belief continued to be so widespread that in some rural regions, even partially naked animals like Lucifer were looked askance at and killed. Payne had never heard of chupacabaras when she gave him his name. He was simply an evil little raccoon. To many other workers, he was also "Bald Ugly Guy."

The real demon in the summer of 2009 was the virus. Lucifer was safe in isolation, but in the main raccoon pens, the disease ravaged the young and the weak, leaving dead raccoons and exhausted, sobbing young women in its wake. Hope for Wildlife had 350 raccoons that year, a record number, and when panleukopenia struck, experts told them to expect a mortality rate of eighty to ninety per cent. The disease is different from distemper, for which it is often mistaken. Distemper is a slow, painful killer. Panleukopenia is quick and very deadly. With distemper, wild animals come out of the woods to wander aimlessly on roads and near people's homes. It is a disease the public can see. With panleukopenia, there is nothing to see.

"Wildlife doesn't even make it to people's yards, so the public never knows it's there," Swinimer said. "It's so quick, twenty-four to forty-eight hours at the most. We'd be feeding them one minute, an hour later they'd be dead. It was so sad. Some days, there would be garbage bags of them. In the end, we probably released as many as we ever did, but only because we started with such a large number."

Once Hope for Wildlife knew what the disease was, they researched, got advice, and put in place a stringent battle plan that required cooperation from the entire volunteer staff. Vaccinations were started immediately. Separation and isolation without interfering with the rest of the wildlife guests used up every inch of available space. Staff used footbaths when entering or leaving infected areas. Clothing could not be worn from one unit to another. Making the sanitation rules even more urgent was Swinimer's discovery that raccoons weren't the only animals at risk. Mustelids, including all members of the weasel family, were also vulnerable. In particular, Swinimer was concerned for the aging pine marten that had for so long been the symbol of Hope for Wildlife's spirit and principles.

"I was really worried about Gretel. I was just panicking," she said. "Any skunks, anything in the weasel family could have caught it."

Working amid the diarrhetic, vomiting, and dying raccoons was not an easy thing for trained professionals, but Swinimer's staff included many young women of high school and college age. One of them was Meredith Brison-Brown, a Dalhousie University student who joined Hope for Wildlife in July and stepped into the tail end of the nightmare. She said the smell of the disease was horrible and constant, and when it came from an animal, death would be right behind.

"There was a foul, bitter odour to it. You couldn't avoid it. The animals' stool would go completely white and they'd lose control of their bowels, then their mouths would dry up. It happened so quickly. They'd be fine one minute, then they'd be gone."

One of the things she noticed was the support the staff members gave each other. She came in just as the outbreak had begun to wane and spent most of her time in the bird room, freeing up senior workers for the raccoons, but Brison-Brown saw what was happening with veteran staff members.

Medical experts couldn't explain Lucifer's lack of body fur. He was simply bald, bad tempered, and knew how to cause problems at Hope for Wildlife.

"Many people were having a really hard time of it," she said. "There was a lot of crying, a lot of hugging going on, and people supporting each other."

Swinimer echoed Brison-Brown. The staff members, she said, were troopers.

"You have to remember, we have young people who have never been exposed to something like this. They were amazing. They pulled it all together," she said. "There were tough times and there were tearful times, but through it all, no one quit and no one gave up."

This support and teamwork allowed them to beat the odds. Statistics said Hope for Wildlife would lose between eighty and ninety per cent of their animals, or about three hundred out of three hundred and fifty. Instead, the staff kept the death rate down to fifty per cent, not only saving half of all their raccoons, but also keeping the virus from spreading to any other species. By late July, it was over and all the animals held in isolation, including Lucifer, were moved back to the main nurseries.

Now that he didn't have to share the spotlight, Lucifer's personality and talent for trouble started to blossom. He easily remained the most bad-tempered raccoon of the year but also began to display his loathing for keepers and their rules through a highly developed sense of the dramatic.

Playful first-year raccoons. There was little play in 2009 when a deadly virus killed half of that year's number at Hope for Wildlife.

"Any time I went near the cage, he would hiss and growl," said Brison-Brown. "Then he would slowly go to the back of his cage and all of a sudden charge the front."

"He made a lot of us really nervous," added volunteer Sabrina Horne.

"Since he was the nastiest raccoon we had, it was naturally Lucifer who figured out how to make our lives even worse by learning how to unlock his cage door," commented Payne.

If there was one animal in the mammal nursery workers didn't enjoy searching for, it was Lucifer, but Payne was right about his abilities and he quickly became an escape artist of renown. The complicating factor was that after he had trashed whatever he could get his paws on, all he wanted was a nice, warm, dark place to snuggle his furless body into. This, combined with his reputation, made for some very hesitant searchers.

"We'd look everywhere for him, all the while slightly nervous he was going to jump out into our faces as we peered under things," Horne admitted.

Tiffany Sullivan remembers one of those incidents. She and Horne had come in early and found the mammal room door properly closed, but Lucifer's cage empty. A cursive search found nothing, and there was no particular mess to show he had been roaming at night, so Sullivan checked the logbook to see if he had died. There was no entry, but given the evidence and the events of that summer, they assumed he had and went about their work. Hours later, as their shift was ending, Sullivan climbed a stool to put some freshly washed towels on a top shelf. Some of the ones already there looked a bit dishevelled, so she started to reorganize them and came face to face with her "dead" raccoon, contentedly asleep at the bottom of the pile.

"There he was! It scared me so badly, I screamed and jumped backwards off the stool I was standing on," admitted Sullivan.

This and several similar incidents turned out to be only warm-ups for the main event. One morning, arriving workers found all the squirrels out of their cages and clinging in terror to the inside of the nursery's screen door. Some thought it was cute, others funny. Then they went inside. What faced them was total destruction. Lucifer had not only set himself free, he had also managed to open every other raccoon's cage.

The raccoons had knocked over the squirrel and chipmunk cages, freeing them and breaking all the dishes in the process. Every shelf and counter had been ransacked and something like

ON THE MOVE

Once solely a North American animal, the highly adaptable raccoon is now found throughout Europe and in Japan. Escape and deliberate releases in the twentieth century account for this spreading, but not its massive success. The raccoon is an animal originally of the hardwood forests, but has shown itself completely comfortable in marshes, mountains, farmlands, and especially cities.

a tornado had swept through the towel case, tossing at random every towel and rag. Lucifer and friends had also territorially urine-marked everything they touched, and according to Brison-Brown, "poop was everywhere." The mayhem had a strange familiarity to it, she said. Unrolled streamers of paper towels were strewn about, cages were overturned, dishes smashed, and animals on the loose.

"It was as if a college party had taken place in there!" she said.

There were no raccoons in sight until someone checked the row of boxes atop their cages. Each one held a sleeping raccoon. Lucifer was curled up in a box containing stuffed toy animals. It took almost two hours to re-cage everyone, clean up the mess, and locate a missing chipmunk which was finally discovered hiding inside the back of a refrigerator. Locks were placed on all the raccoon cages within days.

Lucifer had not only been in isolation because of the virus. There had also been the question of whether his hairlessness could spread to others, so he was without animal friends for a considerable period. Gradually, workers started to feel pity for him. Hayley Inkpen was one of them.

"He stayed by himself for a long time. I eventually started feeling bad for him because the other raccoons had friends to play with, and all he had was a stuffed toy," she said.

"I don't know how or why Lucifer started to become less angry and less of a brat, but I began to notice that he'd come to the front of his cage if I walked by and would look out at me," Inkpen continued. "I started to be able to pet his paws and face through the bars. Next, I opened up the cage, and although it took a few minutes of standing with my hand out, waiting, Lucifer would eventually come up and allow me to pet him. It even got to the point that with much patience, I was able to pick him up a few times without getting bitten or clawed. It was around this time that Lucifer began to gain everyone's sympathy and was given a proper name that sounds much better than Ugly Naked Guy."

About this time, he was reintroduced to other raccoons, but that revealed another problem. Lucifer had forgotten how to get along with peers, and would annoy them constantly, demanding to play when all they wanted to do was curl up and sleep. It was obvious to humans that he was looking for attention, but to his own kind, he was the annoying new kid with no social skills. Eventually he settled in, but not without some tense moments.

Hope for Wildlife's staff gradually became accustomed to Lucifer. His temperament grew better with time and their fear of him waned, but his missing coat stubbornly refused to grow. That constituted a major problem because the purpose of bringing in orphan raccoons each spring was not to keep them as pets; it was to care for them until they could take care of themselves. Each was given the best possible introduction and experience learning to catch food and live as a regular animal that could be placed back into the wild. Lucifer was quick to pick up skills, and based on that should have been ready for autumn release with the rest of his peers, but Swinimer and her crew knew it was not going to happen. No one was going to put a coatless raccoon outdoors for the winter. Until he grew fur, he was theirs, no matter how cantankerous he got.

Every year at the rehabilitation centre, there were a few young raccoons born too late for autumn release. They had to be overwintered, which meant Lucifer would not be alone. Raccoons do not hibernate, but grow a heavy coat and sleep most of the time, sometimes in a deep torpor similar to a bear's. They occasionally eat and come out of their den to look around, even hunt if they are in the wild. Swinimer was very worried about how Lucifer would

Lucifer in all his nakedness.

take the cold weather, but when it came, it appeared to have no effect on him. He didn't have fur, but the rest of the raccoons he was with did, and when they all piled into an insulated nesting box, he seemed comfortable.

"Lucifer lived surrounded by their fur to keep him warm," said Swinimer. "I was really worried, but he did fine. You'd see him out running around on the coldest days. He didn't seem to be bothered by it. His skin is like leather."

By the time his second spring came, Hope for Wildlife faced a decision. It was starting to look as if this raccoon was never going to grow more hair than he arrived with, which meant he was no longer a rehabilitation case. Now they had to decide if Lucifer had enough attributes to merit keeping him as an education animal. Certainly his looks and disposition ruled out work with school children, or even adults. About the only two things he did well were getting along with other raccoons and eating. Swinimer took a hard look and came up with an idea. If he was too feisty and ugly for people, why not let him educate other raccoons?

"He's going to serve a purpose, and we're going to keep him until he sprouts fur or forever, whichever comes first," she announced. "Every year, we have a terrible time teaching our young raccoons how to eat on their own. It's horrid. I don't know why raccoons are so hard to wean. It's like they know how to suckle, but they don't know how to go to the next stage and start chewing. With an adult to teach them and show them through example, it might speed up the process. That would really help us with our workload."

It would also give a bald and occasionally bad-tempered raccoon a place to live and people to take care of him. Perhaps it did not make him any less troublesome to humans, but whether showing raccoon pups how to catch their first minnow in a plastic wading pool or munch down on a tasty June bug, at least now he had a purpose and a home.

CHAPTER 9

A CHRISTMAS PELICAN

Bird watchers love Nova Scotia. Jutting out into the Atlantic as the easternmost mainland of North America, the province has a wealth of regular feathered species, plus other less frequent visitors that can make a birdwatcher's checklist tingle. Western birds occasionally wander east. Infrequently, feathered folk from Europe make a wrong turn at Iceland and stop in for a visit. Birds from the icy north have been known to wander south and, as if to balance that, their cousins who should stay in the warm south get confused and show up shivering in Atlantic Canada. Sometimes these long-distance ramblers are capable of getting back home on their own, but other times their lives are in jeopardy. That's when Hope for Wildlife gets called in.

NIGEL

It was just two days before Christmas and things were slowing down at Hope for Wildlife. Winged migrants had gone where such migrants usually go, towards the sun and away from the cold, while the short days and frigid darkness had driven many fur-bearers into their dens. Those herbivores still awake moved cautiously under the protection of night, afraid to show themselves against day-lit snow. Predators, as always, shadowed them.

This was the season of surprises, and for Hope Swinimer, one came that year from the part of the province where she grew up. A Department of Natural Resources worker in Yarmouth phoned for advice. Traffic was being stopped by a brown pelican in South Ohio on the road to Argyle, Swinimer's childhood home. The bird, said the DNR worker, was standing on the icy highway, looking disoriented and interfering with traffic. His confusion was understandable. Yarmouth, Nova Scotia, in December had little in common with the Carolinas, where he should have been, according to the leg band he wore.

Every year the storms of autumn bring the unfamiliar to Canada's east coast, sweeping southern birds northward, far from their intended destinations. By the time the wind's yearly rampage ends, birds unsuited for the climate often find themselves stranded along the coasts of Atlantic Canada instead of arriving in Florida, Central America, or Mexico. In the past, misdirected egrets, tropical birds, and white pelicans had made their way to Seaforth and Hope for Wildlife for refuge and rehabilitation. However, even compared to them, this brown "Christmas" pelican on a Yarmouth County highway was late—very late.

Swinimer had learned not to let strange avian discoveries on Nova Scotia's shores startle her. She had seen many of them, and sometimes what should have been a rarity after a while became expected. For example, Hope for Wildlife had learned to be ready for an autumn wave of cuckoos, a bird rarely seen in Nova Scotia.

"In the fall of most years we'd get them—hundreds of them—like raining cuckoo birds. I think one year we had almost eighty as patients, all in the same three days. All because of the wind," she said.

For this brown pelican, the October and November storms were things long past. It was winter, not autumn. Swinimer told the Natural Resources worker to capture the bird, warm him up, and get some food into him. When he looked ready, they took him to Hope for Wildlife.

An examination by a veterinarian showed the pelican had no major problems. He was dehydrated and underweight, and a few toes were frostbitten, but these were all things he could recover from.

The warmth of the sun through a south-facing Seaforth patio door makes this a favourite pelican rehabilitation spot.

"Considering the time of year, everything was pretty superficial," Swinimer said. "Some of his nails were in rough shape, but they would grow back out."

He reminded people of the pelican in the movie *Finding Nemo*, so they named him Nigel.

The most exciting discovery about Nigel was that he was banded, and a little searching revealed he had been tagged in North Carolina, just about the northernmost range for his species. For a pelican, he was a northern bird, but that certainly didn't make him a winter bird for Atlantic Canada.

Hope for Wildlife took its time rehabbing Nigel. He needed warmth, rest, and food. It was Christmas and a pelican could not be released in Nova Scotia until at least spring, so there appeared to be no rush. The only major difficulty Swinimer could see was his food. Brown pelicans feed by diving into the water and scooping up fresh fish with their bill pouch. In the frozen North, such a dive would most likely be fatal, so Hope for Wildlife would be the source of the fish he needed.

A TRUE SEABIRD

There are many species of pelicans all over the world, but only the brown pelican lives exclusively on salt water. The American white pelican stays mostly in freshwater habitat, although it usually spends a few winter months on brackish waters. Species of pelicans elsewhere in the world can often be found on brackish or salt waters, but freshwater is their natural home and where they are most common.

"You can have no idea how difficult it is to get fresh fish in Nova Scotia at certain times of year," commented Swinimer. "It's almost impossible. We had to feed him trout, sometimes salmon."

The personality of her new guest surprised Swinimer, who up until then had considered pelicans quite difficult creatures. A white pelican she had once rehabbed before had not been her favourite patient.

"I didn't realize there was such a huge difference between the brown pelicans and the white ones. The brown pelicans are pretty easygoing. In Florida, they hang out with the fishermen, hoping to get some free fish, so they are used to people. This bird was very tame. He would take fish from your hand," she said.

Nigel's unusual presence in Nova Scotia, plus the holiday season and its tradition of little miracles, put him in high demand with media, especially television. His personality on camera guaranteed good coverage. The Christmas–New Year's week is a dead time in newsrooms everywhere. It is when reporters dig through scant possibilities for something unusual that will grab public attention, and there was Nigel, the Christmas pelican. He was an instant star.

"I did at least five interviews," Swinimer said. "He would just sit there. As I fed him fish, I'd talk to the person doing the interview, and the bird was pretty cool, very easy to handle."

The history of the brown pelican in North America has been a remarkable one, in many ways similar to that of the bald eagle. Like eagles and other raptors, this bird was almost wiped out in the United States during the DDT crisis of the 1950s and 60s. Although slowly making a comeback, the brown pelican is still listed as endangered in many areas. Nigel's place of banding, North Carolina, and from there south along the American Atlantic seaboard, was the only part of the species' former range where it remained plentiful. The Pacific and Gulf coasts were hardest hit. By 1970, when brown pelicans were first listed as endangered, not one pair remained in Louisiana. That was both a shame and a point of irony, since Louisiana was known as "The Pelican State."

Today, the brown pelican, like the bald eagle, has made a comeback in some of its former home territories. It is still most plentiful from North Carolina through Florida, a large brown bird with an expandable pouch that dives from high in the air into the water to catch fish. Although it is the smallest of all pelicans, with a wingspan of about two metres, the brown pelican is still a large seabird and popular with tourists. One bad habit it has is frequenting fishing piers, looking for handouts. This often leads to birds getting caught on fishermen's lures, a painful and often fatal mistake. Another problem is that it incubates its eggs by standing on them, which results in a high breakage rate.

The one good thing about brown pelicans being declared an endangered species was that people learned about then, and governments made money available to correct wrongs against them. As a result, rescue and rehabilitation centres for brown pelicans sprang up all over the southern United States. Most of these new rehabs were, like Hope for Wildlife, members of the International Wildlife Rehabilitation Council (IWRC), whose gatherings always featured news on pelicans and their plight.

After she found Nigel, Swinimer remembered meeting at one IWRC conference an elderly man from southern Florida whom everyone seemed to regard as a pelican expert. She found his business card. His name was Harry Kelton, and he was the head of a seabird rescue and rehabilitation facility in Biscayne Bay. She was in luck: his specialty was brown pelicans.

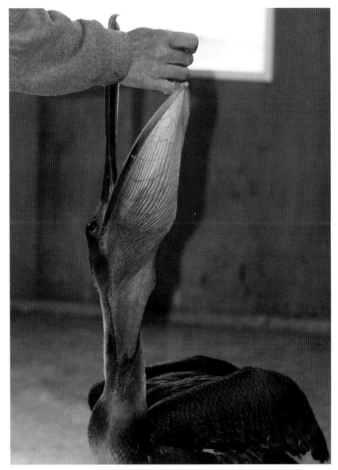

In the wild, a brown pelican's huge bill is used to scoop up fish. In rehabilitation, it's hard to miss when feeding.

"I immediately called him. He was still in Florida and got really excited about the story. He said he would love to have Nigel," said Swinimer.

Harry Kelton was the founder of the Pelican Harbor Seabird Station and a legend in his part of Florida. When he retired as a mechanical engineer at the age of seventy, he and wife Darlene moved to a houseboat just north of Miami in Biscayne Bay. The first thing they noticed there was the appalling number of injured seabirds in the waters around them, so the couple started helping. In 1980 they opened the Pelican Harbor Seabird Station. At first their work consisted mainly of removing fishing lines, lures, and hooks from brown pelicans that had run-ins with fishermen, but they soon expanded and were able to hire staff. One of their major tasks became helping birds stuck by golf balls on southern Florida's many courses.

Swinimer knew if she could get Nigel to Kelton, things would go right for the bird, but the question was how to transport him in the middle of winter. Finally, after much negotiating, she found a solution. If all the needed paper and medical work was done, and the bird properly crated, Air Canada would do the rest. Nigel would be airlifted to Toronto, where the local Humane Society would pick him up at the airport, look after him overnight, and put him on a flight to Miami the next morning. Kelton and his people would meet the plane at the airport and take care of Nigel until he could be released.

The media found out about the new development, which naturally led to more press coverage for Nigel and publicity for the airline. Air Canada knew good public relations when it saw it and charged Hope for Wildlife almost nothing for transporting Nigel.

"They would have done it for free, but they charged me eighty dollars because they didn't want the liability issues," said Swinimer. "If they'd done it for free, they felt they would have been liable if the bird died in flight. I didn't understand that, but they gave me a really good deal."

Articles in the local Florida and Yarmouth newspapers reported that Nigel had arrived well, and was eventually to be released. Carla Allen, writing for the *Yarmouth County Vanguard*, investigated further and discovered that even in wildlife rescue, some government agencies still insist on their pound of flesh.

Air Canada had done its part, putting Nigel on two different flights and getting him to Florida for only eighty dollars. Wendy Fox, a worker at Pelican Harbor Seabird Station, said the staff at the airport cargo depot was "wonderful and cooperative," even waving the standard import fee. However, Fox added that staff at the United States Department of Agriculture were exactly the opposite. They insisted on looking at what was in the box before it officially entered the United States, and despite the fact that it was only 3:15 PM, told her it was after-hours.

"They charged me overtime," Fox said. "They charged me two hundred and fifty dollars to look into the case, say 'That's a pelican,' and fill out the paperwork. That's a third of our fish bill at the moment per week."

Fox said Nigel was placed with some slow-moving birds until his frostbitten toes were completely healed, but after that he was turned loose with the local "rowdy crowd," most of whom were about his age. The biggest concern at Pelican Harbor Seabird Station was

AND THEN CAME RALPH

It was September of 2010 when Hope Swinimer rushed to Dartmouth's Main Street after hearing reports of a pelican there. She had not seen one in Nova Scotia since Nigel had left the province seven years earlier, but Hurricane Earl had just swept through, so anything was possible. Witnesses said the bird had been in the parking lot of Ralph's Place, Dartmouth's best-known adult entertainment venue, but was now on the building's roof. Instinctively, Swinimer took her capture blanket, swung open the front door of Ralph's, and asked to go up to the roof. A startled clerk called for the manager. Patrons began to stare and chuckle, and Swinimer quickly became aware of her situation: a strange woman with a blanket trying to talk her way into an adult entertainment facility claiming to be looking for a lost pelican—a bird that as far as anyone knew, didn't live in Nova Scotia.

Thankfully, someone outside called to her that the bird had left, so she departed Ralph's, tracking it to the parking lot of McDonald's next door. It was indeed a brown pelican but before his food. Nigel had eaten from the standard herring menu as soon as he arrived, but Fox wondered if being fed trout in Nova Scotia had left a longing for something tastier. She hoped they could acclimatize him quickly to pelican life in Florida, before memories of Hope for Wildlife's cuisine inspired him to make another northern pilgrimage.

she could act, it flew to the Dartmouth Veterinary Clinic, then to the parking lot at Burger King, where it stole some food and caused traffic problems. Next, however, the bird slammed into the glass front of a nearby building and stunned itself. Swinimer quickly made the capture and took her new guest, now known for obvious reasons as Ralph, to Seaforth for rehabilitation. He was very tired and hungry, but had not suffered major damage. Wendy Fox, who was now executive director of Pelican Harbor Seabird Station, agreed to take him if he was flown to Florida.

CBC Radio's *Information Morning* host Don Connolly knew that unusual wildlife was nothing new for Hope Swinimer, so he decided to take a different approach. In an interview with Hope, he suggested the sequence of moving from Ralph's to McDonald's to Burger King to unconscious on the sidewalk might have a certain familiarity to it.

"Sounds like a Saturday night, doesn't it?" he asked. "Sounds like a bad Saturday night."

CHAPTER 10

BARRED FROM NOVA SCOTIA

Owls are strange birds. They are mysteriously nocturnal, their family tree is ancient and inspires awe, and those big saucer eyes can make a person very nervous. They also seem to come down with strange, undiagnosable ailments that sometimes make a wildlife rehabilitation worker wonder if a feathered wise guy is setting them up for something. Then there are those times when, just as a Hope for Wildlife staffer seems to have an owl mystery solved, something incredibly unexpected and ironic happens, leaving mere humans to wonder if these silent flyers really can see into the unknown. Or if perhaps, just maybe, there is a good reason for those thousands of years of myth and legend.

CLUCKIE

It was a tale that grew with the telling, a story full of all the elements and devices of good fiction. Irony was abundant, as was suspense. The plot unfolded with twists, turns, and surprise shifts in setting on its way to a surprise ending. It had the sweet aroma of a bestseller, perhaps even a Hollywood movie. The fact that it was all true only made it more interesting.

Cluckie was an owl of mystery from the very beginning. Some workers swore he came from the Annapolis Valley, others that he was a local from Seaforth. One volunteer stated flatly that he was dropped off at Hope for Wildlife Society's rehabilitation centre by a hurried someone who would not stay around to fill out paperwork. Another said she thought he was part of a shipment of injured wildlife from the Department of Natural Resources. There was a story that he was found on the ground, thin and weak from hunger, and immediately rushed to Hope for Wildlife, but in another version, someone had him for a week before seeking help when they could no longer get him to eat. The when, where, and how of his origins were only the first items of mystery. His character was also a matter of concern. He clacked his beak and hissed when anybody came near, disliked being handled by humans, got one with his talons if he could, and generally was a cranky individual. Cluckie fully lived up to a great horned owl's reputation for being difficult, a textbook case if there ever was one. The problem was, he was not a great horned owl. Cluckie was a barred owl, one of the night flyers known for being cooperative and gentle, the owls who on occasion, according to Hope Swinimer, actually seemed to like interacting with humans.

Added to identity and attitude was the question of what, if anything, was wrong with this bird, because even when experts near and far got involved, things were about as clear as a mud puddle full of raccoon cubs. He was that kind of a rehab case. Nothing was predictable with him, not the beginning, middle, nor most certainly the end of his story.

One of the few things known for sure was that Cluckie arrived on February 17, 2009. He was emaciated, that was obvious, but whether from lack of food or disease was difficult to determine. A quick examination at Hope for Wildlife could find nothing seriously wrong, but it was evident he was not using his legs properly, so Cluckie was sent to the Dartmouth Veterinary Hospital and Dr. Barry MacEachern for a more detailed analysis. Again, nothing other than his inefficient leg use was found, and he returned to Seaforth in the hope that rest and food would improve things. But they did not.

"He had definitely had leg problems," said Allison Dube, coordinator of Hope for Wildlife. "They were sticking out in front of him and he seemed to have very limited use of them. When you

LEAVING THE NEST

In a barred owl nest, the largest chick will sometimes get rid of food competition by pushing out the smallest. Parents will attempt to feed it on the ground if it survives the fall. All young are out of the nest before they can fly, using their beaks and talons to pull themselves onto nearby branches. This happens at about four weeks, and at this point they become known as branchers. They fledge in the sixth and seventh weeks, but remain in parental care for at least four months.

put him on the ground to let him walk, he sort of shuffled. He just didn't have good grasping ability. He could perch, but I don't think he could hunt very well."

Nothing seemed to help, and in a few weeks he was back at the Dartmouth Veterinary Hospital. The staffs at both the rehabilitation centre and hospital were totally confounded by what ailed Cluckie, knowing only that it seemed to involve his legs, and even then, they could find the symptoms, but not the cause. Something had happened, something that did not show up in an x-ray. Whatever it was, Dr. MacEachern decided to give this owl of dubious origin, character, and health the full diagnostic package, calling on resources outside of Nova Scotia. A blood sample was sent off to Cornell University and one of North America's finest ornithological laboratories.

Hope for Wildlife faced crucial decisions with this barred owl, the same ones that had to be made whenever an animal came in. Could his life be saved? If so, would he ever be well enough to be released back to the wild? Was there another way for him to live usefully if he could not be released? It wasn't often that the organization's trained staff and local veterinarians were together unable to find answers, but this was one of those times. Calling on Cornell was bringing in the big guns, but they were needed.

Cluckie, pictured here doing defensive beak clacking, simply did not like people. This was unusual for a barred owl.

When the results came back, instead of providing clarity, they only made the situation worse. One test had shown positive for the dreaded West Nile Virus, which could have explained the leg problems. However, a different test for that same ailment on Cluckie's blood sample was negative. Either way, a mention of West Nile Virus was not a thing to be passed over lightly, even though no birds had tested positive since 2003 in Nova Scotia. It demanded attention.

West Nile Virus became a major concern in Canada around the year 2000 during a worldwide spread of the disease. It had been carried globally by birds, but did not remain solely an avian problem. Mosquitoes fed on bird blood, then bit people and transmitted the virus to them. Death could and did result. For a while, there was rampant fear of an epidemic in humans. The virus entered Canada in 2001 and was found in birds in Nova Scotia in 2002. There were never any cases of human infection in Nova Scotia, and the risk factor here was always considered very low. West Nile fear lasted almost a decade, but gradually faded, and by 2010, dead birds in Nova Scotia were no longer being routinely tested for the virus. If Cluckie were found to have West Nile in 2009 it would have been urgent news, an amazingly important discovery, especially since owls are known to spend their entire lives within a few kilometres of their birth nests.

However, there had been one positive and one negative test on this barred owl. Nothing had been decided, and both the Dartmouth Veterinary Hospital and Hope for Wildlife needed to be certain before deciding the owl's future. Another blood sample was taken and sent to Cornell, and got lost. A third sample was provided, and to everyone's relief, it tested negative. Officially Cluckie did not have the virus, but the nagging question of why that first test came back positive remained.

There were two schools of thought on West Nile and Cluckie. The first was that he never had it. For that to be true, the first test would have been a mistake, a false positive, a glitch in the system. That sometimes happened and in theory was possible. The second theory, the one Dr. MacEachern favours, was that the owl indeed did have West Nile Virus at one time. Damage had been done, but he had managed to live through the attack and it was almost out of his system when the first test was taken, and completely gone after that.

"We never figured out what was wrong with him. I still think he had West Nile," MacEachern stated. "I believe it went in, did its job on the nervous system, and then when we tested again, we got a negative test because the virus was gone. They can get over it, but by that time the damage is already done. That's what I think happened to him, but we'll never know."

According to MacEachern, a better picture of West Nile Virus and its possibilities in Nova Scotia might have been available if health officials had focused on owls all along. Instead, because they were preoccupied with other birds, ones like Cluckie may have slipped by unnoticed.

"There were never that many reports around here," he said. "Owls are supposedly one of the birds of prey that we see West

LET'S SHOOT 'EM!

In April of 2007, the Bush White House announced a plan to help save the spotted owl by shooting barred owls in the spotted owl's reserved territories. Those areas are West Coast old growth forest protected from logging, and environmentalists who had fought many battles to save those areas saw the announcement as an attempt to shift the blame for the spotted owl's decline so that logging could begin again.

Nile in because of what they eat. They are kind of our sentinels. Everybody was worried about crows and stuff like that, but it should have been owls people were watching."

In any case, the barred owl in question was again back on a regimen of food, rest, and hope for the best. He was, as Dube put it, "in limbo for a while." Cluckie became a resident of Hope for Wildlife's owl attic and over several months showed some improvement. He still could not walk, but had gone from being unable to stand to being able to perch more or less normally.

His wings and flying appeared fine, so out he went to the flight cage, the last step before release. His talons still appeared weak, and the question was whether they were minimally strong enough for him to hunt. If they were, he could be a free bird again. If not, Hope for Wildlife would have to make a decision, the one it was always uncomfortable making. Cluckie, with workers' fingers crossed, was set free twice. The first time was short lived, but the second in November 2009 lasted several weeks and hopes were high that he was living happily as a wild bird. Then one day in December, Cluckie showed up weak and starving on the rehab centre's boardwalk. He did not resist when picked up and penned—a bad sign. Swinimer and her staff faced the unpleasant truth that perhaps they had been trying too hard to avoid the obvious, and now stood nose to nose with it.

Cluckie's new home in Manitoba.

"After that, we knew he just couldn't be able to hunt," Swinimer said. "Otherwise he'd be gone. The only reason he was coming back was because of hunger. We had kept him and kept him, hoping that maybe he would get even better, but it was clear it just wasn't going to get any better than it was."

When a release failed at Hope for Wildlife, the remaining choices were always simple but unpleasant. The creature could either be used in education or euthanized. Otherwise, the rehabilitation centre would have long ago morphed into a zoo packed with crippled birds and mammals.

"We decided that Cluckie could not be released, but also that he would make a horrible education animal. He really didn't like us," Swinimer said.

The dreaded word was sitting there, staring at them. Euthanize. Sometimes it had to be done, but once again Swinimer chose to pursue other options. They had several barred owls still legitimately in rehabilitation that winter, and one more would not break the system. Besides, as long as the bird was alive, there was always hope, no matter how unrealistic.

"We held onto him for the winter because we had a lot of other barred owls. We had space for him, you could say, so we kept him," Swinimer rationalized.

Five months went by and there was no news on Cluckie. No one expected any. He was on borrowed time, or so most people thought, but then on May 27, Dube sent out a staff memo that included this short item:

> The barred owl Cluckie has made the trip to Manitoba! Dr. James Duncan, with the Manitoba Department of Conservation received Cluckie yesterday after a long flight from Halifax. For those who need a refresher, Cluckie is a barred owl that came to us over a year ago. We suspected he might have West Nile Virus, but after several tests and a long wait it was determined that he did not. Still, Cluckie's legs were not 100% and although a release was attempted, it was unsuccessful. Cluckie was deemed non-releasable and we're quite certain that he is unable to hunt due his limitations with his legs. Dr. Duncan will be studying Cluckie's molt patterns and vocalizations to better understand barred owls and try to figure out where they are living in Manitoba and why their numbers are scarce there.

Dube had been working quietly for about two months on a way to save the apparently doomed barred owl. Dr. Jim Duncan, zoologist, one of Canada's most respected owl experts, and author of *Owls of the World*, had contacted a number of Canadian rehabilitation centres looking for a non-releasable barred owl to use in his work. Hope Swinimer had received the message and passed it on to Dube, who immediately thought of Cluckie.

"We basically had an owl sitting in our attic that we didn't know what to do with," Dube said. "I contacted Jim and we talked. In the end, we decided that Cluckie would be appropriate for his purpose."

Duncan is internationally known for his twenty-five-year study of Manitoba's provincial bird, the great grey owl, and as a prolific author. He understood what Cluckie's situation had been in Seaforth.

Renowned owl expert Dr. James Duncan and the bird he made his life's work, Manitoba's great grey owl.

"It's inevitable that some euthanasia is necessary," he said, "but when there is an opportunity, is it ever wonderful to work collaboratively and have the good folks at Hope for Wildlife, Allison in particular in this case, be able to respond and help us out. And it's a commitment. If Cluckie's going to be helping us, my opinion is that bird has a government pension plan of sorts. As long as I'm alive, it's going to be well taken care of."

According to Duncan, exchange efforts such as this should be made more often because "there is a really important role for this unreleasable wildlife, and the opportunity exists to use them." Being able to "supplement and complement our field research" by examining their own permanent sample of a species has huge benefits.

"I know from my experience that studying wild owls is great, but you often get to hold them in your hands once, maybe twice. So we can learn a lot from having an unreleasable barred owl in captivity."

Swinimer acknowledged that Cluckie, after all he had been through, appeared to have found a permanent home with a quiet environment and not a lot of disruption. It was just the type of life he

THE LANGUAGE GAME

The word owl came to English from Anglo-Saxon, and from there can be traced back to older German sources. In early English, it was *oule*. The old German word was *ule*, which became the modern *eule*. Both languages are thought to have taken their original word from the ancient Germanic *uwwalo*.

needed, "plus he'll be helping the barred owls in Manitoba, which is really exciting. I think he'll have a really good home."

The barred owl is a relative newcomer to Duncan's province. It is an eastern species, but due perhaps to human change in forest cover, the owl moved west through Ontario and across the prairies in the 1960s. Based on calls heard at night, Duncan and colleagues know "we have a pretty healthy population of barred owls here in Manitoba" but have little detailed knowledge on nesting, habitat, or food. They have fallen behind neighbouring provinces and recently began a study to catch up. There is a sense of urgency, as the barred owl's move west has put the endangered northern spotted owl at increased risk. Both are creatures of old growth forest, and the more aggressive newcomer is pushing spotted owls out of their territories. They are genetically similar, resulting in some crossbreeding and the creation of what are being called sparred owls or botted owls.

There is also the matter of the interloper's potential effect on Manitoba's great grey owls. In his twenty-five years of research, Duncan saw only one case of a female great grey on her nest within the territory of a barred owl.

"I found her dead at the bottom of the nest tree with two talon-sized puncture marks in the back of her head," he said.

The great grey is slightly larger than the barred, but their talons have about the same span, and a barred owl's are much thicker and stronger. That means the new arrival can take a much greater variety of prey than the great grey, which catches almost exclusively field mice and shrews.

As Manitoba's scientists study the barred owl and its new importance in their province, Cluckie will help Duncan and his staff get to know his kind. They plan to record and study his calls, looking at inflections and, perhaps, regional dialect. Duncan hopes to form a molting template so that when a feather of a wild barred owl is found, they can determine the age and time of year when the bird lost it. Most importantly, Cluckie will be there as questions arise in Manitoba about his species, and will be living the good life as a ward of the province. Not bad at all for an owl from Nova Scotia with an indiscernible past, shaky health record, and dubious future back home.

CHAPTER 11

BUT IT WAS WORTH A TRY

There are not that many moose left on mainland Nova Scotia. They were once the prime game animal and the largest creature in the provincial forests, but that has changed. In a period of less than one hundred years, they faded and were gone, leaving greying racks on sheds and camps as reminders of what they once were. The mainland moose fell victim to habitat change as well as a disease carried by the white-tailed deer that came and flourished in the changing Nova Scotian landscape. There are still a few mainland moose, mostly in Guysborough and Colchester counties, and it has become a major event to see one. If what you come across is a calf, it is even more exciting. Or at least it should be.

ESTER

How young is too young? For a wild animal, is there an age below which attempting to save its life is folly? If the chance of success looks slim, should a potential rescuer forget what they have seen, walk away, and let nature take its course? Such decisions are always difficult and can raise a crop of trying emotions. By 2009 Hope Swinimer, founder of Hope for Wildlife, had been in the wildlife rescue and rehabilitation business

FEW LEFT

Environmental change and disease have almost wiped out the moose population in mainland Nova Scotia. It is listed as an endangered species. A recent survey estimated the population at only about one thousand animals, despite a complete hunting ban.

for twelve years, returning more than 1,100 creatures to the wild each year. She had taken over new and challenging programs from other agencies, including the care of both white-tailed deer and raptors, and won a major national environmental award for her work. However, Swinimer had always quietly longed to test herself as the rescuer of Nova Scotia's biggest land mammal. She wanted a moose.

Joy should have been in the air, then, the summer night she and companion Reid Patterson returned home to find a hobbled young moose in the middle of the Seaforth rehabilitation centre's driveway. But two major problems tempered the delight. One was that the moose was only three or four days old, the umbilical cord still attached. The other was a dream-shattering shot of reality: Hope for Wildlife lacked a provincial permit to keep moose.

Ester, as she became known, was not in good shape. Swinimer later learned she was part of a sad scene encountered a few days before by a couple who were out for a woodland walk when they witnessed a cow moose struggle to birth twins.

"The first baby moose was born, and that was Ester. Then they watched the second one start to be born, and it got stuck. They immediately ran and called the Department of Natural Resources, and were told to just leave it alone, let nature take its course," Swinimer said.

The couple did as they were told, but passed a sleepless night. The next morning they returned to find the mother dead, her second calf unborn, and a bedraggled Ester still standing there. Despite the advice of Natural Resources, they intervened. The living calf was taken to their home and fed cow's cream. After a few days, it was obvious something wasn't working, so the animal was dropped off at Hope for Wildlife. Ester's major problem was not one that anyone could fix. She had not received colostrum, a special kind of mother's milk produced for newborn mammals that creates a baby's immune system and jump-starts its digestive tract. In an emergency, colostrum from cows or an artificial substitute can be used, but the window for the calf to absorb it is very small. It has no effect after forty-eight hours, very little after twenty-four, and for full effect, it must be received within twelve. By the time this calf arrived at Swinimer's rehabilitation centre, more than three days had passed. It would be another two weeks more before Hope for Wildlife fully understood Ester's background, including the missing colostrum.

"We knew then the odds were stacked against us," Swinimer said. "It's really hard to save an animal that's had no colostrum whatsoever. It helps deal with the simple, everyday things that life throws at it, and without it, their immune system is severely compromised and they really have a very difficult time. They can get through a couple of months, but things knock them down and take hold, and they have nothing to fight them off with."

Despite what appeared to be a hopeless case, Swinimer and her staff decided not to give up. However, the problem remained that Hope for Wildlife had no provincial permit to handle a moose.

"I immediately called the Department of Natural Resources to get permission," Swinimer said. "They said I could have her for one week. I was very disappointed with that, and I just expected any day for DNR to roll in, get Ester, and take her away."

Swinimer says she blames herself for what followed. She took Natural Resources at their word and did not prepare for long-term care of the moose calf.

"I feel responsible in a way for some of Ester's hard luck. I keep thinking that if I'd known I was going to have her for two months, I would have researched. I would have known things. But I kept asking myself what was the sense to get special pellets in, what was the sense for doing all the research, if she was heading up to the Shubenacadie Wildlife Park almost immediately? I feel very bad that I didn't do my homework, no matter what I'd been told."

After three weeks went by, Swinimer began to question whether DNR was still planning to come for Ester. Then she switched into high gear, researching and ordering the special foods that might have increased the calf's chances if she had received them almost a month earlier. Swinimer quickly discovered that what she required was available, but not readily. It was several more weeks before the supplies arrived.

"It was just a calamity of errors," she said. "I wasn't prepared, I hadn't researched, I didn't think I'd be able to keep Ester for more than a week. But all that said, in all honesty, I don't think it would have made any difference in the outcome, because of the lack of colostrum."

Ester did not go down without a fight, and the Hope for Wildlife workers admired her for that. Four times each day, she would drain two or three bottles. She began browsing. The workers, realizing grass was not natural moose food, began scouring the woods and marshes of Seaforth for plants that were.

"We were picking her water lilies and stuff she'd find in marshes, trying really hard to get the proper foods into her. We gave her the best possible chance, but one day she just took a turn," Swinimer said.

Ester spent her final days at the Metro Animal Emergency Hospital in Burnside where she received round-the-clock veterinary care. "I'll always remember walking her in through the waiting room. It was full of people with dogs and cats, and little children asking 'what's that, Mommy?'" Swinimer remembered.

Ester made several trips in and out before her last stay and Swinimer said the staff gave every effort they had and more. But Ester just kept getting worse. Every day while she was back at Seaforth, the doctors from the emergency hospital would come out to treat her, and so would the technicians. As long as Hope Swinimer believed in a miracle, everyone did, and no one spoke what they knew to be the truth: this was one they could not, would not, win.

"We had her on all kinds of drugs, at least she was comfortable," said Swinimer. "I just didn't want to believe she wasn't going to make it, I just wanted so badly for her to live."

Lack of colostrum and proper early diet were the main factors blamed for Ester's death. The special moose food finally arrived but it came too late to be of use. Despite the fact that she had no way of

Rehabilitation worker Hayley Inkpen introduces Ester to her aunt.

knowing Hope for Wildlife would be Ester's home for life, Swinimer still blamed herself because she didn't follow her instincts and start a long-term rehabilitation program at once. She has always believed that if DNR had acted on the day Ester and her struggling mother were first discovered, the calf, at least, would have lived.

"To me, there is one argument I will never understand from government and that is to let nature take its course. I hear that so many times from them. To start with, what we deal with are usually human-wildlife conflicts in nature: things that we have caused, things we have a responsibility to fix," said Swinimer.

Swinimer said the moose birth was an example of what she thinks is official policy gone wrong.

"Everything we do as human beings interferes with nature. We drive our cars to work, we pollute, we over-consume, we over-popu-late—so why is it okay every single day to negatively impact nature but not to positively interfere when we have the chance?" Swinimer asked. "If I was a DNR employee who received the information, I

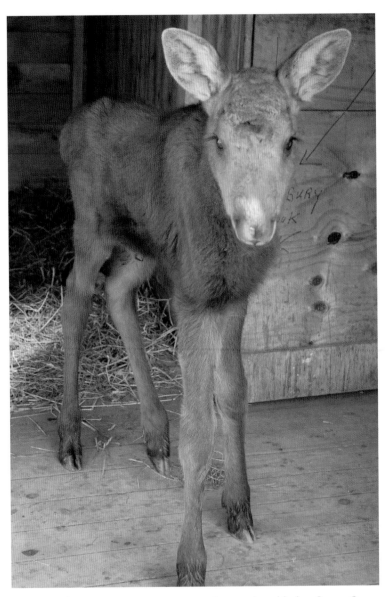

Ester: without an immune system, she was lovable but doomed.

would have been right there. I'm not a vet, but I'm sure we could have got one and saved that second calf and perhaps the mother. The twins both could have gone happily ever after with their mom. If the cow died, we could have at least got the milk, we could have got the colostrum."

THE ORIGIN OF THE WORD "MOOSE"

Early explorer Thomas Hanham reported in 1613 a large deer-like animal called *Mus* in the Abenaki language of New England. By 1616, more famous explorer Capt. John Smith was referring to the animal as a "Moos."

In this case, it was not human action but rather inaction that killed a mother moose and her two calves.

"The only reason those people kept that little moose was they didn't want to see it die. They kept it because they cared and they knew the government would come to destroy it. There is no reason in the world Ester should have died, none. Cow's colostrum would have worked every bit as well. I've got freezers full, but it won't be absorbed after forty-eight hours. There is no sense giving colostrum once the animal is past that point," Swinimer said.

The story of Ester is a bitter one for Hope Swinimer and her staff. They believe that every wild life is precious and worthy of special effort, even if the case genuinely appears hopeless. But this animal could have been saved, Swinimer felt, and there is no loss greater than that.

CHAPTER 12

WITH A LITTLE HELP FROM HER FRIENDS

Many organizations and individuals are empowered either by regulation or conscience to help wildlife in crisis. The problem is getting the help where it is needed, when it is needed. An eagle caught in a bobcat snare needs help immediately. A fox kit mauled by a dog doesn't have to bleed to death, but probably will if the right people don't know about it. Only very rarely do concerned individuals, private help groups, and government agencies all fall into place to create the perfect support system for an injured wild animal. When that does happen, the story is worth telling.

DUNLOP

Why the turtle had attempted to cross Purcell's Cove Road in Halifax was unknown. It was later discovered she was pregnant, so perhaps she was looking for the right type of gravel to nest in. One of the sad ironies of turtle life is that as humans alter stream beds and destroy natural nesting places, they often create long, narrow replacement gravel banks nearby, called road shoulders. Unfortunately, these are usually attached to roads, and with roads come cars. The result is that

The Oaklawn Farm Zoo's 'Northwest Turtle-tory' has been home to all four types of Nova Scotia's freshwater turtles. The zoo has a turtle hatchery nearby.

every summer across Nova Scotia, roadways are littered with dead pregnant turtles.

This one was a wood turtle, an at-risk species classified as endangered in Canada and vulnerable in Nova Scotia. A city street at any time of day was not its native habitat.

Wood turtles are commonly found in the St. Mary's River watershed of the province's northern mainland and in some parts of southern Cape Breton. There are a few other pockets, but none near Purcell's Cove Road in Halifax. A human likely found it in the wild, brought it to the city, and either released it or let it escape. This is unfortunately very common. In fact, it is a major cause for the species's decline. Wood turtles spend a lot of time on land during the summer months, and while they are faster than other more plentiful turtle types, such as the snapper and eastern painted, they are still not speedy enough to escape curious human hands.

The motorcycle policeman on traffic patrol did not see who hit the turtle, just the cars swerving to avoid something in the road. But when Sgt. Michael Spearns arrived, he saw it was a turtle.

NOVA SCOTIA TURTLES

There are four species of turtles found in fresh water in Nova Scotia. The two most common are the eastern painted turtle and the common snapping turtle. The other two are at-risk species. The wood turtle is classified as vulnerable, while the Blanding's turtle, found only in the vicinity of Kejimkujik National Park, is threatened.

Her injuries were serious, with both the upper shell (carapace) and lower shell (plastron) smashed, but she was alive. He knew that without an intact shell to cushion the blow, a second strike would be fatal.

For most turtles on summer roadways, this would have been the end of the story. Shoving her off the road so cars avoiding her did not cause an accident would have been the normal thing to do. However, this turtle was very lucky. Sgt. Spearns respected wildlife, and he called in a nearby cruiser and sent the turtle to the Spryfield Animal Hospital. Before doing so, Spearns took a guess at the make of the offending car tire and based on this named the turtle Dunlop.

A person who cared had been in the right place at the right time, so good things started to happen for the turtle. The support structure was starting to come together.

The Spryfield Animal Hospital saw Dunlop needed help, but crushed turtles were not something they had experience with. Plus, it was evening and they were getting ready to close. Something had to be done quickly, so they phoned the person they knew could help. Hope Swinimer was at her day job as manager of the Dartmouth Veterinary Hospital. Swinimer said the staff at her hospital knew how to repair broken turtle shells and that Dunlop should be transferred.

"We've had probably half a dozen turtles over the years, and Dr. Ian McKay has patched them up," said Swinimer. "Mostly painted turtles and snappers. This was our first wood turtle."

A baby wood turtle fights its way into a world where it is an at-risk species.

Delivering the turtle to Swinimer was not going to be easy. It was getting late and neither hospital was open overnight. Enter the Metro Animal Emergency Clinic in Burnside who agreed to take Dunlop, keep her comfortable, and get her to Swinimer on their early morning shuttle.

"They sent it over, we got it, and Dr. McKay x-rayed it," said Swinimer. "That was when we found out it was female and pregnant. We were really excited. He went to work on her right away and patched up the shell as best he could. I think he used stainless steel wire, mesh, and epoxy on that one."

The procedure was not short. It took about ninety minutes, but McKay declared it a complete success and Swinimer removed Dunlop to Hope for Wildlife's Seaforth facility for rehabilitation. It was at this point that *Halifax Chronicle-Herald* reporter Josh Visser and photographer Eric Wynne entered the picture. Word of Sgt. Spearns's unusual rescue had spread and the newspaper wanted a story. The article ran on the front page on Thursday, July 5, two days after the accident. Spearns was quoted as saying that as a traffic cop he was usually "after the hare, not the tortoise" and he was glad to help because "the poor thing would have been squished if we hadn't been able to get her off the road."

WHY A SNAPPER GETS AGGRESSIVE

Three of the four types of freshwater turtles in Nova Scotia can withdraw themselves between their upper shell (carapace) and lower shell (plastron) for protection when threatened on land. A snapping turtle cannot. Its lower shell is much too small for that. Since it is also too slow to flee, a snapper has only one means of protecting itself and that is to threaten a fight. This accounts for its reputation as a nasty character.

Dunlop stayed about a week at Hope for Wildlife. Swinimer had heard about someone who knew more about wood turtles than she and her staff, an Annapolis Valley turtle expert named Mike Brobbel, Curator of Reptiles at the Oaklawn Farm Zoo near Aylesford. With the wood turtle now improving and carrying eggs, she felt his care was what Dunlop needed. Swinimer phoned him and he agreed.

Brobbel's main concern was for Dunlop's eggs. Her shell had been fixed in Dartmouth, but she had undergone considerable trauma, and the question now was not when she would lay the eggs, but if she would. He placed her in their turtle enclosure with a number of other wood and painted turtles.

"I kept an eye on her every day because I knew she was full of eggs," said Brobbel. "She needed to get rid of them before she became egg-bound. That's a very serious situation with turtles if they don't lay their eggs in time."

Turtles frequently die from this condition and there are many causes. If the eggs are too large or if the turtle is injured, she cannot lay them. If the desirable nesting gravel is not available, she will not nest. If she has suffered a traumatic shock, she will delay until she feels better. Dunlop had suffered all three.

For several days, Brobbel watched and worried over Dunlop, hoping for the best but fearing the worst. What finally happened was somewhere in the middle.

INTERNAL COMPASS?

Wood turtles are said to have a pronounced homing instinct. In an American study, one turtle was released more than two kilometres from its home water. It made it back in five weeks. One particular Nova Scotian wood turtle travels annually between its hibernation site and nesting bed, a distance of seven kilometres by water or five overland.

"Because she wasn't in her natural environment, she was having a hard time of it. She didn't seem very comfortable about digging a nest. What she ended up doing was just laying the eggs on the open ground," explained Brobbel.

It had been estimated in Dartmouth that Dunlop had about ten eggs. Brobbel managed to save three, but two were already collapsed and past hope.

"One was pretty fresh, so I got that into the incubator. We ended up hatching out a baby," he said.

Long before the new wood turtle entered the world, its mother was gone. Thanks to Visser's story and Wynne's photographs, Dunlop had been transported to her home, her real home, Pictou County's East St. Mary's River. *The Chronicle-Herald* put the story on the front page where it was hard to miss, and in widely separate parts of the province, two biologists involved in the preservation of wood turtles had seen it.

In Halifax, the story made John Gilhen curious. The former curator of the Nova Scotia Museum of Natural History, Gilhen was a wood turtle expert, and he knew the turtle wasn't where it was found of its own volition. When he saw Wynne's photos, his curiosity surged. Gilhen recognized the series of small notches filed into the edge of her shell as a code, indicating she had been catalogued and had a numbered file with the Nova Scotia Department of Natural Resources. Not only would they know who she was, Dunlop could be placed back in her original home water system.

These newly hatched snappers will grow to be the largest freshwater turtles in Nova Scotia.

Meanwhile, Natural Resources regional biologist Mark Pulsifer was reading his morning paper in Antigonish. "I looked at the front page of *The Chronicle-Herald* and I noticed that the turtle had been notched," said Pulsifer, who worked with a summer university crew and was in charge of the wood turtle research project on the St. Mary's River. He could take the animal's identification even further than Gilhen.

"As soon as I saw it, I knew it was one of ours," he said. "One of my summer crew had captured that turtle at some point in the past, and put a very distinctive notching pattern on its shell."

Each notching pattern was unique and corresponded to a file number which held data gathered on the turtle. Pulsifer was certain, and a browse through his records proved him correct: Dunlop was an East St. Mary's River turtle, and he knew exactly what stretch of water she came from.

The irony was that she had not been caught and catalogued as part of a survey. A motorist had found her next to a highway and brought her to Pulsifer's project. In 2005, as in 2007, she had been

All freshwater turtles bask on sunlit days. A wood turtle, shown here, basks further from water than other types.

drawn to a road shoulder to look for the kind of nesting gravel she had trouble locating in her native habitat.

"She was definitely looking for a nesting site," Pulsifer said. "As a rule, the females are trying to find a certain consistency of sand and gravel, and often that stuff on the side of the road is the perfect thing. It's not uncommon at all in the area I'm in charge of to see wood turtles up on the side of roads, trying to dig holes."

According to Pulsifer, roadside nesting endangers the wood turtle population and not just because of highway traffic.

"There's a double jeopardy in the sense that if cars don't get them when they're along the road, something else will. They nest at night, and raccoons like to follow along the roadsides at nights. They'll sniff out the nests, dig them up, and consume the eggs."

On a rainy day in August, Dunlop came home. Gilhen had picked her up at the Oaklawn Zoo and driven her from Aylesford to Antigonish. From there, a group that included Gilhen, Pulsifer, and a small entourage drove to the roadside riverbank where she had been picked up and released before. It was the kind of place wood turtles love: a clear river winding slowly through prime agricultural land. About a month later, her one surviving hatchling also made the trip and joined her.

Pulsifer believes what happened to Dunlop is important because it shows there are people who still care about wildlife. Humans caused her to suffer, and yet so many other humans were determined to set this right that it got done with almost impossible efficiency. That, said Pulsifer, was not just a statement about the potential of wood turtles as a species. It was also a statement about our human potential.

CHAPTER 13

ADAM AND THE CHRISTMAS GLOVES

To many of the First Nations peoples of North America, an encounter with a great horned owl was a sacred moment. Called "magic maker" by the Creek nation, this fiercest of all owls was considered to be in touch with the spirit world, but would only give its advice to the holiest of medicine men. To other First Nations peoples, only a very powerful spiritual leader could touch a great horned owl and not be attacked by it. Medicine men often wore the owl's feathers to show their connection to it, and to many nations great horned owls were conduits for souls.

ADAM

"This owl certainly has an attitude," Hope Swinimer commented.

"You couldn't pay me enough to pick up that bird," someone else said after looking at a picture taken by passerby David Chaisson of Ketch Harbour, who just happened to be out on Cole Harbour's Salt Marsh Trail that day.

It was January 1, 2010, and the comments were about a great horned owl found injured that afternoon on the abandoned rail bed that forms the trail. How this most dangerous of all Canadian owls came off the marshland to Hope for Wildlife's shelter has left many who heard the story in awe, and a few shaking their heads in disbelief.

The great horned owl is large, powerful, and known to be aggressive towards humans. Its talons have a crushing power of 500 pounds per square inch, the greatest of any North American bird. Compare that to 60 pounds for the hand of the average adult human male. It will defend its territory aggressively against any creature, no matter the size, especially during courting in December and January or in February when nesting begins.

Of course, all predators are territorial to some degree, and this protective instinct doesn't make the great horned owl a woodland monster. It's just an owl being an owl, with its own manner of doing so.

However, that manner has often been called ferocious, earning the great horned owl the nickname "The Tiger of the Night Sky." The other large owl in Nova Scotia, the barred owl, will quickly become a meal for any great horned that can catch it. For that reason, barred owls, themselves territorial, regularly clear out of their hunting range the moment a great horned owl moves in. Its reputation makes the great horned the only owl in North America said to have killed a human. There's debate over whether that claim is true or false, but the simple fact that so many believe it helps explain why the story of how the owl dubbed Adam was rescued that New Year's Day has a special edge.

The hero was Steve Mitchell of Lawrencetown. He, with partner Mary Leigh Petersen and dog Geisha, were out to work up an appetite for New Year's dinner. Usually, they stopped at the first of four bridges on the abandoned rail bed that carries hikers across the marsh, but the weather was good so they decided to go further, hoping to see snow buntings. No buntings were spotted but there were more clamouring crows than usual, and at first they thought nothing of it. They were about halfway across the old Cole Harbour dykeland and as they approached the next bridge the dog began to bark at something in the rocks. It looked at first like a porcupine, but then they realized it was a puffed up owl. Its hissing and bill-clicking told them it was injured and wanted them to stay away.

Rescuer Steve Mitchell and a great horned owl named Adam, moments after meeting.

Their first reaction was to call Hope Swinimer, but there was no answer. They left a message, and thinking that would take care of it, resumed their hike. Immediately a raucous mob of crows began circling the owl menacingly and the trio returned to see if they could help it. After several tries, Mitchell, using Peterson's down vest as a wrap, gently captured the injured owl. It was then, according to Peterson, that they realized their situation.

"We found ourselves back on the causeway with an owl wrapped in an Eddie Bauer vest, cradled like a baby in Steve's arms, with its talons encircling his fingers and its beak six inches from his face," she later wrote to Swinimer. "I must add here that Steve was wearing his new MEC, good to minus seventeen degrees, gloves. The label said nothing about carrying owls. We were over three kilometres from the car, with really only one choice. We headed to it."

It took about half an hour. Swinimer had got the message and called to say she would meet them at the other end, while the owl gradually stopped its warning clicks and hisses, and, according to

OWLS IN NOVA SCOTIA

The great horned, barred, and saw-whet are Nova Scotia's most common owls, but the long-eared owl, short-eared owl, and boreal owl also breed in the province. Barn owls are becoming more common and may breed in Nova Scotia. The snowy owl's winter visits can fluctuate from rare to infrequent, depending on its northern food cycle. Three others, the eastern screech owl, great grey owl, and northern hawk owl, are rare visitors.

Peterson, "seemed to enjoy the ride." However, it kept an eye on the dog, and Mitchell slowly became aware he was losing sensation in his fingers.

Swinimer was waiting in the trail-end parking lot. They had told her on the phone that Mitchell had picked up the bird and was carrying it, so she expected a mild-mannered barred owl and the sight of a glaring great horned surprised her. What was really amazing was that even though Mitchell had not restrained the bird's talons, the usual first step with this type of owl, the captive was sitting calmly on Mitchell's hand without crushing it. Swinimer decided it would be best to get the owl off its rescuer before something happened to change its mood.

She placed a blanket over it, which relaxes most wild creatures, then had Mitchell extend his owl-clad arm into a transport basket. Unfortunately, a great horned owl can be unpredictable and Swinimer had misread this one. The owl had already been relaxed. When the blanket went on, the bird tensed and once it felt apprehension, brought all its tremendous crushing power to bear on Mitchell's hand for the first time. His reaction was instant.

"This really brought Steve to his knees," Peterson said. "Actually, I think he had his forehead in the gravel and was rocking back and forth, all the while trying to relax his hand while the owl tightened its grip."

This female barred owl fostered a pair of great horned owl chicks. They eventually outgrew her, never discovering that their "mom" should have been their meal rather than their protector.

Swinimer then told Mitchell that when any bird of prey, including this owl, locks its talons, they cannot be forced to release, adding that she had seen people pass out from the pressure.

However, logic suggested that if the owl had been relaxed before the blanket went on, removing it might solve the problem. The crisis was over as the bird released Mitchell's throbbing hand, jumped to the ground, and made a hopping run for it, with Swinimer in close pursuit. After a short chase, she made the capture and took the bird to her Seaforth shelter for examination.

Its left wing damaged, a great horned owl later known as Adam tries to hide amid the rocks along Cole Harbour's Salt Marsh Trail.

Swinimer called him Adam because another great horned who had come to her on Christmas Eve after losing a few rounds with a porcupine had been named Eve. It turned out Adam's wing was badly bruised but not broken. He also had some broken tail and primary feathers, which would need to grow back before release. That was expected to take some months, but in fact the feathers looked much worse than they actually were. They were just badly mussed, nothing a good preening could not straighten out. In less than two weeks, once the swelling in his wing went down, Adam was released back to Cole Harbour Salt Marsh.

With great horned owls, releasing them back into the environment they came from is crucial for several reasons. They are territorial but keep a rather small home range, only a few square kilometres at most. They are fierce protectors of that area, especially in mid-winter, which is their mating season, so an owl released far from home will try to get back to where it belongs before its territory is lost to another male. Even though a male owl has proclaimed his territory, he will not keep it long if he is not there to defend it. There is, however, a second and related reason. Owls mate for life, and great horned owls in particular are highly protective of their partners, with both males and females ready to attack and fight any creature that threatens the other. During nesting season, they are driven by the need to be with their mate. For a great horned owl, this creates a problem much greater than simply finding the correct direction home. In order to get there, it will have to cross the territories of other owls equally protective and fierce.

Exactly what had happened to Adam that day was unclear, but his wing injury was the type that usually came with a collision. The best guess was that Adam was chasing something that flew under the bridge and clipped the structure trying to go under it. The bridge was the only thing within hopping distance of where he was found that afternoon. Great horned owls are classified as nocturnal, but will hunt in the low light of a fading mid-winter day, which means the damage was likely quite recent when he was found.

In the end, Adam's injury was no more severe than the one he gave the man who rescued him. Steve Mitchell went to hospital for a checkup and a tetanus shot because, as Peterson pointed out, owl talons are not kind to human hands. Nor, she noted, to expensive new Christmas gloves you have just been given. It was little solace to Peterson when Swinimer later told her that she and Mitchell, without any of the proper gear or training, had brought in not only the most feared of all owls but also "the feistiest great horned I've ever seen."

Needless to say, the couple's New Year's dinner was late that year.

CHAPTER 14

THE FOX WHO STOLE HEARTS

In folklore, no animal is as omnipresent as the fox. Its slyness is legendary, its charm magical. When a beautiful woman is called foxy, it is an echo of the ancient archetype of shape-shifting vixen who transform to become attractive human females, irresistible in their appeal. There is an ancient Chinese belief that a fox may take human form at age fifty. By one hundred, it may have knowledge of things a thousand miles away, and at one thousand years, become the celestial fox, beyond human control and communicating directly with Heaven.

SWEET PEA

Martinique Beach wraps itself around the Atlantic Ocean in a gentle curve of almost five kilometres. It is the longest white sand beach in Nova Scotia, home to beautiful dunes and endangered wildlife. In the spring of 2001, it was also the temporary home of an orphaned red fox, a small orange stranger too young to be on its own, cowering under a boardwalk for shelter, safety, and the picnic scraps it scavenged for food.

The phone rang at Hope for Wildlife.

"Look, there's a little fox here on Martinique Beach that seems to be in distress," the man on the other end told Hope Swinimer. "Its mom was killed by a car and everybody's been feeding it. It's just sort of hanging out. Can you do anything for it?"

Swinimer was concerned, but not overly so. This was the first she had heard of it, and the founder of Hope for Wildlife had long ago learned that one call usually doesn't guarantee an emergency. As it turned out, that call was just the start and the emergency was real.

"My phone just continued to ring after that, call after call after call, all about this little tiny fox pup, so then I was getting concerned," said Swinimer. "We were thinking about sending a trap down to see if we could catch it. From what the callers were telling me, it sounded like it was way too young to be there on its own."

Things developed quickly from there. The very next day, Swinimer received a call that a German shepherd had attacked the kit, leaving it injured and in desperate need of help. The man who called said he'd be happy to watch a live trap if Hope for Wildlife would lend him one. Within hours, the trap was set up at the beach.

"I'll always remember. It was seven o'clock Sunday morning, a beautiful summer morning in early July. He pulled into my yard and opened his trunk as I started down to meet him. Then he reached in and pulled out the saddest looking fox I'd ever seen. That little fox was no more than two pounds, and looked near death at that point. She couldn't use one of her hind legs at all."

This was Sunday and Swinimer immediately started stabilization procedures that would keep the kit going until she could take her to a veterinarian Monday morning. She warmed the little fox up and got some fluids into her. A lot of people, she said, harm an obviously thirsty and malnourished baby animal by giving them milk first.

"I didn't start her on milk right away because that's the worst thing you can do with a dehydrated animal. It's essential to rehydrate them first," explained Swinimer. "We did that for about twelve hours, then gave her just a little bit of milk that night. The next morning, we took her in to the Dartmouth Veterinary Hospital."

The little fox had been bedding down in a thick growth of beach pea under the seaside boardwalk so Swinimer named her Sweet Pea. The x-rays did not look promising and it was obvious

ABOUT FOXES

In a family history going back forty million years, foxes can track a genetic connection to wolves, coyotes, dogs, and jackals. There are five or six species of foxes in North America: red fox, grey fox, arctic fox, swift fox, kit fox, and possibly the island fox. Only the first three are plentiful.

this fox was a mess. Dr. Ian McKay could tell the animal suffered from rickets from its poor diet in the month spent on the beach. Sweet Pea had been fed or scavenged leftover junk food, not a good diet for a growing fox, and the result had been a crippling lack of vitamin D, the cause of rickets. The things Dr. McKay found wrong were serious, long term, and not curable. There were growth problems in the spinal cord, calcified discs, leg bones that weren't developing properly, and from what he could tell, this fox was in serious pain. Swinimer decided to put her on pain killers and see if rehab would help, but even she, who always hated the idea of euthanizing, knew that the possibility of not saving this fox was right there, staring at them.

"We tried so many things to get Sweet Pea back up and going, and there were many times we thought we should probably euthanize and give up on her," she said. "She was in pain, and even though we had her on pain meds and tried to make her comfortable, it was difficult. For about four months, we tried to get her to use her leg and not walk with her back all hunched up. We even had acupuncture done on her. There was only one vet in the area doing acupuncture at that time and that was Dr. Laura Lee. She did a wonderful job, and the acupuncture actually seemed to give her some relief."

Nothing could be done about the malformed leg bones. They simply had not grown properly, and no amount of rehabilitation would change that. Despite everything that had been done medically,

Sweet Pea, Hope, and a young admirer.

Sweet Pea still could not use her right rear leg. It was a ticking time bomb, and one day in early fall Swinimer was home and busy when she heard an unearthly wail coming from Sweet Pea's pen.

"I ran down to the enclosure, and somehow she had broken, totally snapped off, her hind leg," Swinimer remembered. "She was just screaming in pain. We rushed her to the Dartmouth Veterinary Hospital."

Dr. Paul Robb was on duty. He took one look at Sweet Pea, then at Hope, and said what she didn't want to hear: "Hope, we should euthanize."

He had always been against keeping a wild animal if it could not be released. It was not that he believed wild creatures should go unaided, but he felt that if they were meant to be wild, they should be wild. It was obvious now that nothing could ever be done to make Sweet Pea into a wild animal. The leg damage was beyond repair.

COYOTES AND FOXES

An influx of coyotes is bad news for foxes. They compete for the same food in the same habitat, and the larger, stronger, and faster-breeding coyotes will kill or drive out a resident fox population as they move into an area.

"This leg just could not be fixed. Our surgeons are great at orthopedic work, but there was no way to repair this leg. Because of the rickets, the bones were just too weak. To be honest, I guess we'd known all along that her whole life would be a struggle in some way," Swinimer said.

Why didn't she put her down? Swinimer had been asking herself that over the previous four months. Dr. McKay had told her to do it the first time he saw Sweet Pea. Things had not only failed to improve since then, they had gotten worse. Now Dr. Robb was recommending it again. It seemed a simple and obvious decision, but to Swinimer it wasn't. There was something about this little fox that made her hesitate, even then.

"Normally, we would never have gone to this degree, but there were a number of factors that played into it," she said. "First of all, there was the emotional side. She was beautiful, and comfortable around people. She would look at you and seem to be saying, 'Help me!' It was amazing how she interacted with all the volunteers. No animal had done it the way she did."

There was something else, though. In just half a year, she had become a star.

"Sweet Pea had this huge fan base out there, all down the Eastern Shore," explained Swinimer. "Everybody loved Sweet Pea, everybody was talking about Sweet Pea. I'd get dozens of calls every month asking how Sweet Pea was doing. They were from people who knew her at Martinique, and friends of people who had known her at Martinique. People just knew her. She was a famous fox."

Dr. Robb knew Sweet Pea's history. He was aware Swinimer and her people had been working very hard to save her, that the community loved her, and also that she was an extremely easy-going little fox, so he finally gave in and amputated the leg. Everyone waited to see how the long-suffering little animal would react, and were overjoyed when suddenly she began to thrive.

"She got along really fine, even great, on three legs," Swinimer said. "It seemed like from that point on, her life became much better. Her health improved, everything overall was better for her. She was playful and filled a really important role at the rehabilitation centre."

Swinimer had hoped to use Sweet Pea to educate people about foxes and their place in nature, and this became an important part of her work at Hope for Wildlife. However, during Sweet Pea's second spring the staff decided to see what would happen if they placed her with the unruly crowd of orphaned kits, the "foxes in boxes" that required so much of their attention each year.

"We were quite nervous because we didn't know whether it would be a good thing or not. There was always the chance that she would kill them," Swinimer said. "We got her doing that right away, and it just went so beautifully. There was a lot of vocalization at first, but then they started to play and interact, and we knew everything would be just fine."

Workers said it looked like a den mother laying down the rules for the new bunch of kids. The vocalizing was mostly hers, the little ones taking it in, a bit unsure. Swinimer said it was impressive.

"If you've ever heard foxes talk, it's really cool!" she added.

Fox pups are close-knit families who need that dominant influence of an adult, and Sweet Pea filled this important role for all the fox pups at Hope for Wildlife up until the last summer of her life. Every year she'd get ten or so pups to oversee, play, and interact with, and every fall, all the little foxes would be released, and she'd be left behind. The Hope for Wildlife workers always wondered about that. These had not really been her kits, but they were like adopted or fostered children to her, and the staff believed having a family one day and none the next must have had some effect.

"We always noticed for a week or two after they all left, she'd be really quiet and aloof, and we never knew whether she was just

Every spring, about a dozen fox kits arrive at Hope for Wildlife. They are a handful for human workers, but during her stay, Sweet Pea kept them in line.

glad to have the kids out of the house, or if she really was lonely and missed them," Swinimer said.

Even in the long fall and winter months without little foxes around her, Sweet Pea was never alone. Everyone who visited the Hope for Wildlife rehabilitation centre wanted to see her, and with every tour that came through, she was always the centre of attention. The question of when they were going to see Sweet Pea was always on someone's lips, especially with school groups.

"All the kids knew her, everybody knew her. She wasn't always the favourite animal, but at the end of each tour I'd ask the kids who their favourite animal was, and nine times out of ten, they'd say Sweet Pea," Swinimer remembered. "She won the hearts and souls of so many people."

Everyone wanted a photograph of Sweet Pea, and film crews on the Hope for Wildlife site for news or features always seemed to find a way to include a clip of her. Her image started popping up in strange places. On one occasion, someone faxed Swinimer a poster from an anti-fur farming group that had started appearing on walls,

REMEMBERING A FOX

"The one thing I will always remember about Sweet Pea is that she was unlike humans who dwell on the small things in life. She had only three legs but went about every day like she had all four and not a care in the world. If you didn't see her up close, you would have no idea she only had three."

—Sabrina Horne, Hope for Wildlife worker

bulletin boards, and lampposts in the Halifax area. Swinimer had to look twice. It featured a photograph of her fox.

"Did you know Sweet Pea was the poster child for the anti-fur movement?" was the message with it.

Swinimer hadn't known.

"It was a big poster, bashing fur farming, and it was Sweet Pea's picture. They'd been out to the farm one time. But it was tastefully done, and I quite liked it, because it was Sweet Pea. Of course, she was so photogenic that her pictures ended up all over the place. That's why you have to be careful when people take pictures. I like to authorize things like that," she said.

With any wild animal, no matter how long they have been held or how drastic their handicap, there always remains the instinct to escape. Sweet Pea was no different from the others and she got out several times. An organization like Hope for Wildlife, which relies on a large volunteer staff, affords ample opportunity for a wily animal to study its keepers and over time identify the ones it thinks it can pull something over on. Sometimes, they will almost seem to have a thing for escaping on a certain volunteer. With Sweet Pea, that person was Hope for Wildlife's longest serving staffer, Ronda Brennan, the person Hope Swinimer has relied on for years and refers to as "my rock."

Brennan had a deep affection for the fox.

"What I remember most is her sweet nature, and how she'd come for you to scratch her neck because she couldn't do it herself

Foster mother Sweet Pea gets affection from a late-summer kit.

with a missing back leg. You'd give her a scratch, and could see her hip moving where her leg had been."

Trust did not come quickly or easily with Sweet Pea, according to Brennan. Shy at first with almost everyone, she would peek out and watch carefully from her little shelter until she was sure. Then, if you were lucky, she might let you scratch her.

"She escaped on me at least twice, though," said Brennan. "The first time was my own fault for not obeying one of the basic rules."

It was early in her stay in Seaforth and the fox was penned next to a group of raccoons. Brennan had opened the door and leaned in to do something, but glanced at the other animals, not focusing on Sweet Pea, and the fox shot past her. Brennan instantly knew what she hadn't done, and with a fox, even a three-legged one, it only took an instant.

One of the things that won Sweet Pea the hearts of visitors was her ability to pose for a perfect photo.

"I didn't go in and shut the door, I just leaned in, and she slipped right under the door and past me. And she was gone, out of the big barn and everything," Brennan said. "She came and went until they put food out and caught her."

Swinimer said Sweet Pea had a habit of lulling workers into a false sense of security. She was a real escape artist, deceptively quick, who never took her eyes off the door. It was a total mistake to look at her standing in her pen on three legs and think of her as handicapped. Volunteer Bobby Wilson agreed.

"The one thing I will remember about Sweet Pea is the picture I have in my mind of her running as fast as she could up the hill at the farm after she had just been let out by mistake," Wilson said. "You couldn't see that she only had three legs, so she didn't look 'disabled' at all. Fortunately, she came back after four or five days, very hungry and very tired."

The escape of any animal is a serious matter at the Seaforth facility. It backs onto wild country that calls to those in the pens, but if an animal has the ability to survive there, it would already have been released. This was always a worry for Swinimer. While part of her wanted to see all of her charges back in the wild, another voice told her that releasing them to certain death would be even crueler than captivity. She knew, for example, that Sweet Pea, on three legs and with no hunting skills, would have a very short life outside. After the first few escapes, however, she felt a bit more secure about the fox than she did with other animals.

"I always worry about my captive animals because I have such mixed feelings," she explained, "but the part that always impressed me with Sweet Pea was she never went far, and she always came back. We didn't need to live trap her. She'd just return, we'd hold out our hand with a piece of meat, she'd come on over, and we'd pick her up and pop her back in her unit. She'd stay away sometimes for a full week, though. I think she'd go out, have her fun, and then home she'd come. She always knew where her meals came from."

By the summer of 2009, it became apparent that Sweet Pea was not herself. She was eight that spring, entering old age in the world of the fox. In the wild, foxes can live up to ten years, but few make it even close to that, most only lasting two to four. Disease, highway accidents, and hunting take a heavy toll. This was the first year Sweet Pea would not tolerate the newborn foxes she had always been so excited about. She grew quieter and more reclusive as the summer slipped by, and as autumn came, she was no longer eating well.

By Christmas, the end was near, and just after the New Year, Sweet Pea was rushed to hospital. For the third time in her life, a doctor said there was no hope and that she should be euthanized. This time there was no argument.

"I knew how many people loved her, so I took her back to the farm for a few more days for goodbyes, with the full intention of euthanizing her on the Thursday," Swinimer said. "I was just giving everyone a chance to come over and say goodbye, and a lot of people did get that chance."

In the end, Sweet Pea avoided for a third time what she had avoided twice before. On the Wednesday afternoon, volunteers Bobby Wilson and Karla Henderson were with her and Henderson, a former nurse, saw that she was dying. The two women put her in a container and started driving to Dartmouth so Swinimer could say her farewell before it was too late.

On Main Street, only a few blocks from the Dartmouth Veterinary Hospital, they were pulled over for speeding. Henderson frantically tried to explain to the metro police officer that there was a dying fox in the back seat and they had to get to the veterinary hospital. The young policeman had no idea what he had on his hands and just kept repeating "Are you going to cooperate or not?" refusing all requests to look in the container. According to Henderson, by the time he eventually let them go, ten minutes had passed and Sweet Pea was gone.

When the ground thawed in April, Swinimer buried Sweet Pea at the farm, in her wildflower garden. A worker at the hospital had taken a ceramic paw print to be used as Sweet Pea's grave marker.

Henderson commemorated her with this poem:

RUN, SWEET PEA, RUN!

This is the time of year you most notice a fox,
a wily orange blur past white snow and dark spruce
writ large in our consciousness:
Kit. Swift. Cape. Silver.
Cunning King in Luke 13.
Vulpes vulpes for the scientist.
Reynard for the English folklorist, *Regin* or vixen for the German.
Disney caricatures for Robin Hood and Maid Marion.
The Fox! In Stravinsky's *Renard*, and barter for the Voyageurs.
These are people's foxes.

But you, Sweet Pea?

You've made us fox-people for nine years.
A jetsam orphan on the Eastern Shore, bedding down
on wild pea under a boardwalk;
a Shepherd is your second foe,
rickets, your third, and you lose a leg.
Amid this chaos, you must wonder Is this life? Is anybody there?
Hope arrives with meat and mice and might
and before long, the word gets around of
a little orange *piñata* brimming with treasures.

    Oh! The hats you don:
    Mama tutor to young kits,
      patient for the most part with all those foxes in boxes.
    Star attraction for old and young
      who chant your name up the drive with great anticipation.
    Favourite resident for volunteers
      searching for your acknowledgement, carting your cuisine closer:
    Oh, hello, you greet them as gentle as your footfall.
    A fugitive, three times busting out of Dodge;
    we fret daily, nightly: Is she back?

Mostly, though, you rescue us—
From thinking that society and nature have nothing in common.
From thinking there is no such thing as love at first sight.

Thank you, fearless little friend.
Long may you run!

Karla J. Henderson
January 2010

IMAGE CREDITS

ACKNOWLEDGEMENTS

Arcadia Entertainment
Blomidon Naturalist Society
CBC Radio
Dartmouth Veterinary Hospital
The Daily News
The Eastern Gazette
The Halifax Chronicle-Herald
Hope for Wildlife Society
Metro Animal Emergency Clinic
Nova Scotia Department of
    Natural Resources
Oaklawn Farm Zoo
The Yarmouth Vanguard
Adrianna Afford
Chelsea Boaler
Ronda Brennan
Meredith Brison-Brown
Mike Brobbel
Laura Bond
Tamara Cantrill
David Chaisson
Jo-Ann Chinn
Jen Costello
Karen Damtoft
Allison Dube
Dr. James Duncan
Deirdre Dwyer
Eva Mari Sporsheim Gundersen
Karla J. Henderson
Sabrina Horne
Christina Hunt
Hayley Inkpen
Dr. Kathy Lamey
Dr. Laura Lee
Shannon MacDougall
Dr. Barry MacEachern
Dr. Ian McKay
Rebecca Michelin
Janet Mills
Andrea Mosher
Barry and Helen Nicholson
Riley Olstead
Nicole Payne
Leigh Peterson
Mark Pulsifer
Sara Seemel
Emily Ann Seman
Tiffany Sullivan
Hope Swinimer
Tricia Travers
Megan Vaughan
Jackie and Robert Verge
Bobby Wilson

ABOUT
HOPE FOR WILDLIFE

Hope for Wildlife was established in 1997 as The Eastern Shore Wildlife Rehabilitation and Rescue Centre, Nova Scotia's first private organization for the care of injured and orphaned wild creatures. Its existence as a charitable society allowed founder Hope Swinimer to assemble a volunteer staff and accept individual and corporate donations to develop and then expand services. Its home facility at Seaforth is fully licensed and inspected, with a federal license for the rehabilitation of sea birds and a provincial one for indigenous wildlife. The group's name was changed to the Hope for Wildlife Society in 2005. The society's staff, supported by local veterinarians, rehabilitates and releases more than 1,500 birds and animals each year.